_LF_

MICHAEL SANDERSON

WHAT'S THE PROBLEM HERE?

Time-Saving
Problem-Solving Techniques
for the Manager

Executive Enterprises Publications Co., Inc., New York
Prentice-Hall, Inc. Englewood Cliffs, New Jersey

Printed in the United States of America

Library of Congress Cataloging in Publication Data
Sanderson, Michael, date.
  What's the problem here?
  1. Problem solving. 2. Management   I. Title.
HD30.29.S262   658.4'03   81-17801
                                         AACR2
ISBN 0-917386-51-5
ISBN 0-13-952515-7 (Prentice Hall)
ISBN 0-13-952507-6 (Prentice Hall: pbk.)

Contents

MICRO-STRATEGIES

Introduction

When we experience problems, whether in the bustle of managing a business or in the drama of personal relationships, we are generally not able to, or unwilling to, consult a book on problem solving. Usually time and patience are too short at such points for us to begin learning a new technique or exploring a new approach to communication. We manage our problems as best we can, without systematic help.

Unlike many books on problem solving, which present only a generalized methodology, this one is designed as a ready reference manual to be dipped into when you find life presenting you with confusion and difficulty. The book's purpose is to guide you quickly from your initial feeling of being all at sea to a plan of action for tackling your problem.

Many books describing techniques and methodologies are available to help you solve quantifiable and recognizable, though complex, problems. Some of the hardest work in solving problems, however, comes in trying to figure out what is going on, what you should be trying to do, and how you might begin to do it. This book is designed to bridge the gap between the natural unease, disorientation, and puzzlement you feel when first suspecting or discovering a problem and controlled and competent action in solving it.

You will not find in this book detailed solutions for every problem from how to improve productivity in a manufacturing industry to how to discover true love. Nor will you find merely an outline of a problem-solving methodology that leaves you to decide how to apply the techniques in the unique situations of your daily life. Instead, the book is designed to guide you

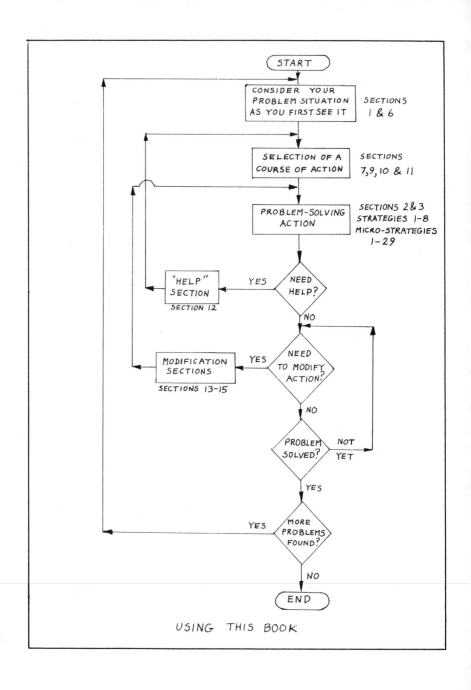

USING THIS BOOK

through formlessness and ambiguity toward recognizing your problem's shape, and on, toward choosing a procedure for tackling the problem from a selection of twenty-nine small, general problem-solving strategies and eight larger ones. In this way you are shown how to move through the difficulties of not knowing how to proceed, and are assisted in finding a strategy to direct your actions in approaching the problem. This is done by means of questions, rather than instruction, intended to guide your thoughts to an exploration of the key areas of your situation.

The diagram opposite shows the basic procedure for using this book. The first step is an initial review of your difficulties in Section 1. If your situation is unclear, Section 2 or 3 will help you clarify it. If your situation is clear, Section 6 will help you decide whether to take a large-scale approach to solving the problem (Section 7), or a small-scale approach (Section 9). If you choose a large-scale approach you will be directed to the strategies. If you select a small-scale approach you will usually be directed to the micro-strategies.

The strategies are complete, problem-solving frameworks designed to fit a specific type of problem—a fuzzy one, for instance, or a complex one. The micro-strategies are much smaller procedures that cover such aspects of problem solving as setting objectives or having a bright idea. Whenever you get into difficulties you can go to the "HELP" section (Section 12), which will assist you in getting back on course. For a more detailed discussion of the book's structure, turn to Section 4.

Three stories are included in the book. "Is the Dam Dangerous?" (Section 5) deals with problem definition and illustrates the use of the questioning technique. "An Interlude for the Weary" (Section 8) deals with restoring self-confidence. "Getting to the Root of It" (Section 16) is a story about problem solving in the steel industry. The story illustrates some of the complications that confuse attempts to resolve difficult issues.

You can use the book in several ways, according to the needs of the moment. You can work through the book from the beginning, or go to the "HELP" section, or find a description of your difficulty in the index, or devise your own approach. Whatever your procedure, whatever your need, you should be able to find advice that enables you to begin tackling your problem. As you define your problem more clearly, you can find guidance for most problem situations and stages. Your approach can be as long or as short as you choose. The book is designed to permit all kinds of chopping and changing of the approach and yet still lead you to a resolution of your difficulties.

It is often hard to know where to make a fruitful start with a problem. Some exploration and false beginnings are inevitable in fuzzy situations. Don't be discouraged if you don't get it all straight the first time in the approved textbook manner. Life isn't often like that. Discarding false leads and making mistakes are part of learning about a problem and can be interpreted as progress. So don't despair. This book can help you at the various stages along the way.

There will be times when you are confronting a situation so confusing that you don't even know how to think about it. There will be times when so many problems clamor for your attention that the biggest problem is finding where to start while there is still time to do something. This system offers assistance for such cases. It also provides help for the times when the situation is clear but you need a more structured approach to the problem. For all cases, a step-by-step procedure for analysis of your difficulty is available to guide you toward the best strategy. So let's move on to Section 1 and take a look at what is happening to you.

First Choices

If you've used this book before and are in a hurry, go straight to the quick-reference index of difficulties and strategies, at the end of the book. Otherwise, choose one of the following two descriptions and proceed as indicated. As you move around the book, make a note of the section numbers you pass through and the strategies you use so that you can easily retrace your steps if necessary.

1. *You have some idea of the shape of the problem or what you want to do, though your idea may be fuzzy and you don't quite know how to proceed.* Go to Section 4, "Some General Remarks on Problem Solving."

2. *Your idea of your problem is sufficiently unclear that you need help in beginning to come to grips with it.* Read on.

Let's look at your difficulties more closely. Which of the following statements most clearly describes your situation?

1. *You are caught up in a crisis situation.* Go to Strategy 7, "Crisis."

2. *A crisis situation is close at hand.* Go to Micro-Strategy 23, "Avoiding a crisis by tackling something concrete."

3. *You feel confused about the problem situation, or puzzled by the events, or you're losing your grip on the situation.* Go to Section 2, "An Uncertain Situation."

4. *You are becoming distressed; you're under great pressure; you feel you are losing control of everything, including yourself.* Go to Section 3, "Things Are Really Getting out of Hand."

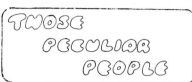

THOSE PECULIAR PEOPLE

OH MY. I'M RUINED, AND I PLANNED AHEAD AND USED THE BEST STRATEGY I COULD FIND

BUT DID YOU KEEP IT UNDER REVIEW?

I WAS TOO BUSY. IT HAD ALWAYS WORKED BEFORE

WELL, YOU SHOULD WATCH YOUR STRATEGY AS WELL AS THE WORLD

IT'S LIKE THE EXPLODING TOMATOES

YESTERDAY'S DINNER, TODAY'S DISASTER

An Uncertain Situation

Clarifying your difficulties can often be quite hard, especially as reason, emotion, beliefs, and aspirations often intermingle and obscure the real problem. Sometimes trying to come to grips with your problem can get you into deeper trouble, placing you in a shifting flux of ideas, attitudes, facts, fictions, and values. You may feel as though you're inside a rapidly changing kaleidoscope of doubts and formless worries.

The advice, strategies, and micro-strategies contained in this book are designed to help you with some of the more difficult things you must do to clarify your situation. What are these tasks? One is to look at how you are coping with the problem situation as a whole. Another task is to examine the problem itself and see what is a part of what else, or overlaps with it. A third task is to see at what different levels things can be viewed. Accomplishing these tasks in an organized fashion, calmly, without skipping around like a panicked steer, should help you to gain a feeling for a systematic approach to the problem.

After some systematic thinking about your problem, you may want to sleep on it. Letting it all soak in during a good rest can be a productive way of tackling a tangled situation.

The following list of headings contains descriptions of some difficulties that you may be facing. Read through the headings until you find the one that most closely matches what you feel. You may find more than one. Then turn to the instructions and information given under the selected heading. If you don't find a heading you can use, you may find something helpful in the quick-reference index of difficulties and strategies at the end of the book. Or, try turning to Section 6, "What Kind of Situation Are You in?" for a different way of looking at your problem. For a refresher on what problem solving is all about, read Section 4.

HEADINGS.

    2-1. You think you have a problem, but you're not sure.

    2-2. You don't know what the problem is. You can't figure out what's going on.

    2-3. You know what the problem is, but you can't find where to start.

    2-4. The problem keeps changing shape.

    2-5. The situation doesn't seem anything like what you first thought it was.

    2-6. You are overwhelmed by detail and need to consolidate. There's too much going on.

    2-7. You are losing your grip on the problem situation. You are floundering.

2-1. You think you have a problem but you're not sure.
It isn't always easy to recognize a problem, or to know whether or not a problem is real or important. You may be feeling suspicious of a placid situation, or sensing that things are too good to be true. You may just be feeling uneasy but unable to pin down the symptoms. You may be sensing potential problems, or you may be worrying unnecessarily and reading things into a situation.

Problem awareness, or problem recognition, is an important part of problem management. This sensitivity to problems and potential problems is a skill, or an art, that you can learn with practice. You can develop a keen nose for trouble, as well as an ability to avert the trouble before it starts. Such a skill is useful not just in watching out for problems, but in seeking out flaws in what would otherwise appear to be a good problem solution. It's not much use solving one problem only to unleash a dozen others in the process.

The following questions comprise a strategy intended to help you to pin down the elusive situation that's causing your unease. This strategy is the same as Micro-Strategy 7.

MICRO-STRATEGY: WHAT'S GOING WRONG HERE?

1. Why do you think something is going wrong?

2. What seem to be the symptoms?

3. Has something changed to cause this feeling of things going wrong? Or, is it the way you are handling things? Or, is there some other cause?

4. Has the situation already changed in a manner that's difficult to recognize? Is the situation different even though it seems the same?

5. Has the situation remained fundamentally the same despite apparent changes?

6. What else is going on? Is it significant? Can you connect your situation with this other thing going on, either by discovering subtle links or by making an innovation?

7. What seem to be the issues or factors involved?

8. Which things are symptoms and which causes? Are some of the things you think are causes really symptoms?

9. Would a single explanation be sufficient, or are several things amiss here, and perhaps presenting a confused picture?

10. Where else could you find information about this situation?

11. What sources that you've never thought of, or heard of, or that you have previously considered and rejected, might be available?

12. What might happen next? In the near future? In the long term?

13. What are the different shapes the future might take? What actions might trigger these future events? What information would indicate the direction being taken?

14. Are you considering which ideas your information supports, and which ideas it does *not* support?

15. Are there any odd coincidences?

16. Is there a common thread running through all your problems? That is, are all or many of your difficulties related in some way?

17. Could you find a pattern by altering your viewpoint or changing your expectations of this situation?

18. Could somebody be misleading you? Accidentally? Deliberately?

19. Might you find a pattern by delving into the assumptions, beliefs, concepts, or values with which you are approaching this situation and life in general? Can you examine the context in which you are setting all this?

Now you should be in a better position to decide whether you have a problem or not. If you are convinced that you do, your next step is to define the problem clearly. You can do this by using one of the problem definition micro-strategies such as Micro-Strategy 4, "Basic fact finding," or Micro-Strategy 5, "Defining, interpreting, and diagnosing the problem." Look also under "Defining the problem" in the quick-reference index. If you think you already have a fair idea of the problem, you may prefer to move to Section 6, "What Kind of Situation Are You in?" for a wider selection of approaches to your problem.

2-2. You don't know what the problem is. You can't figure out what's going on.

Perhaps you can't make the right moves in your work, profession, or private life. Perhaps your spouse, companion, or family has suddenly and inexplicably changed or turned unpredictable, and everything you do makes things worse. Maybe your business or other competition continually outmaneuvers you, appearing where you didn't expect it, or is stronger or faster. Maybe you are trying to figure out the source of a mysterious toxic effect or a strange disease with inconsistent and baffling effects.

The key to the approach required in these situations is heightened awareness, a quality that can improve your ability to seek information, to assess, and to predict. How do you achieve this increased awareness? Briefly, you should proceed along the following lines. Carefully analyze your objectives for the situation and blend this analysis with an exploration of events that demonstrate the type and extent of the problem, its present configuration, its history, its possible and probable futures. This phase requires much weighing and sifting of evidence. It calls for an ongoing questioning of assumptions and for imaginative thinking as you seek further information and other perspectives. It also demands a sensitivity to changing circumstances and their meaning. Only when you've made a rigorous exploration of the problem and your involvement with it will you be in a position to start solving the problem. There's nothing to beat familiarity with the situation, combined with an imaginative eye for fresh perspectives.

To begin your exploration, follow the small strategy given below, which is the same as Micro-Strategy 28. If you want to give your situation a little more thought, turn to Strategy 5 and use parts 3, 5, 6, and 7. If you think a better description of your position would be *intractable*, that is, not easily managed or manipulated, incomprehensible, unstable, rapidly changing in shape and activity, then go to Strategy 8.

MICRO-STRATEGY: FOR A FUZZY OR CONFUSING SITUATION.
The major effort in fuzzy and confusing situations goes into
clarification. Clearing up the confusion requires finding out
what is going on and what the events signify. It means pondering the ideas and categories involved. In addition, it means
finding out what other people are thinking and why, and noting
your own perceptions and thoughts. Make sure you pin the situation down and ascertain why it is confusing.

1. Why do you think you have a problem? What seem to
be the symptoms?

2. What seems to be happening? What difficulties does this
cause? What opportunities does this present?

3. Where are the areas of confusion, fuzziness, or difficulty, or where do they seem likely to be found?

4. What do you already know about this situation? What
could you quickly find out?

5. Is there anything that you're not sure about or that you
don't know?

6. What bits and pieces do you think are involved in this?
Which ones are important?

7. How complex does this problem seem to be? Can you
break it up into smaller parts and then deal with the parts
separately to avoid being overwhelmed by the details?

8. What are the most critical or noteworthy aspects of this
problem? Why?

9. Can a core of difficulty be identified?

10. Which part of your problem is most disturbing and
why?

11. Where else could you find information about this problem?

12. How is this situation developing? What is its history?
What could its future be? How many different ways could
it develop in the future?

13. How do the components and participants of this problem seem to be tied together? What are their interrelationships? Is anything missing?

14. What can be inferred from what you have learned so
far? Where might this lead?

15. Does this raise any deeper issues?

16. What do you understand by the terms, concepts, or ideas that you are dealing with, by the viewpoints you are expressing, by the questions you are asking?

17. Are you confusing any categories or types of things, mixing things that don't belong together in your scheme? Apples and oranges, for example, are sometimes different (one is citrus, the other not) and sometimes the same (both are fruit and grow on trees).

18. Are you setting out with a wrong idea of what is, or should be, going on?

19. What hidden or unstated goals or directions might there be?

20. Is dealing with the situation primarily a matter of getting organized, of making plans, of establishing priorities?

21. Should you seek information, find out where everything fits, or weigh, sift, assess, test, or diagnose?

22. Should you invent something, or produce a new plan or idea?

23. Can you see decisive patterns in growth or change rates and directions, in components or factors, or in their interrelationships?

24. Is there a common thread running through all of your problems? That is, are all or many of your difficulties related in some way?

25. Might you find a pattern by altering your viewpoint or changing your expectations of the future or of this situation?

If you now have a clearer perception of your problem, go to Section 6. If you are still in difficulty, try Strategy 5, "Fuzzy," or 8, "Intractable." or go the quick-reference index, or turn to Section 12, "HELP."

2-3. You know what the problem is, but you can't find where to start.
Some problems are fairly obvious. What is not so obvious is how to tackle them. World disarmament, food shortages, natural catastrophes, marital difficulties, office politics, are all problems of this kind. Often in such situations an indirect approach is necessary. The size and complexity, or the sheer obstinacy,

of the problem may not permit the head-on approach we so often take with our difficulties. Sometimes a back-door route can lead to a solution. Finding such a route requires some exploring. If you try to find different ways to look at the problem, different ways it fits into its context, or different ways the problem is related to other problems around it or to yourself and your attitudes, you may come up with an interesting restatement of the problem—perhaps more than one. You may produce a different view of the requirements for a solution or action plan. It can also be helpful to take a look at the underlying value systems and assumptions, both in yourself and in the situation under study. You may alter your view of what the objectives of any action plan should be. If you can reexamine your problem in any of these ways, you should discover a wider and more imaginative range of possible solutions.

To follow these suggestions, you must be creative and flexible. If you're feeling highly emotional or pressured, look at Section 3 before you begin work in this section. Or, if you're having trouble getting started because you feel disorganized, look at Section 2-6. Otherwise, try the following little strategy designed to help you change your perspective. This is the same as Micro-Strategy 10.

MICRO-STRATEGY: SEEKING A CHANGE OF PERSPECTIVE.
Figure out what you are trying to do, and where you are currently looking for answers. Then see if you can shift your perspective so that you can look for answers in new places, at new levels, or in a different state of mind. A fresh approach is important if you are to find workable alternatives.

1. What are you trying to do?
2. What will be your signs of success? How will you decide when you have resolved things?
3. Can the problem be split up into distinct categories, parts, or areas of difficulty?
4. Do any of these categories or areas reveal interesting side issues? Can you focus on these? What does the problem look like from that vantage point?
5. How would the French, the Italians, or the Russians deal with this problem?

6. What might a blacksmith, a doctor, or a sailor have to say about it?

7. Can you see one point that might be easier than any other to find out about, tackle, or control? Can you do something about this?

8. What are you assuming about the background against which this difficulty is happening? Are your assumptions valid?

9. Can you change your view of how this situation fits into the larger picture?

10. Is there another place you could start?

11. Is there something engrossing you can do to put this problem out of your mind for a while? If so, perhaps when you return to the problem you'll feel refreshed and see the situation differently.

12. Can you start at the end and work backwards? Can you turn the problem upside down?

13. What other situations can you find in which the principles are similar to the principles in this one?

14. Are you looking at this problem in different ways, on different levels? Have you considered such aspects as organization, aesthetics, personality, timing, information, motivation, effort, production, or finance?

15. Does thinking about the preceding list of aspects change the way you see the problem?

16. What psychological or emotional blockages or blind spots in yourself or in others may be involved?

17. Are there any odd coincidences?

18. Who could give you another outlook on this situation?

19. How could you solve this problem in a magical world? Does this solution give you ideas for working on the actual problem?

20. What is the most absurd solution you can think of? What is the craziest thing that could happen? Does this give you any sensible ideas for working on the problem?

21. Can you change the context of your problem?

Now you may want to look at Micro-Strategy 9, "Having a bright idea."

If you have gained a clearer perception of your problem, go to Section 6. If you are still puzzled, try Micro-Strategy 3, "Organizing to tackle a problem."

2-4. The problem keeps changing shape.

Sometimes the patterns, shapes, and trends underlying a problem are elusive. Events can continually surprise you. Dealing with this kind of problem can be like trying to predict the weather thirty days from now, or the state of global politics one year hence. In such a case, the problem will continue to change its apparent shape because you are working with a situation for which nobody has yet devised concepts or techniques for resolution. Perhaps you have not taken sufficient care, or have not had sufficient opportunity, to analyze, to find the basic difficul-

ties and determine their relationship to each other and events surrounding the problem. Or perhaps the underlying situation you had once perceived has changed without your being aware of it.

Your main concern should be to seek out a central pattern or patterns, to find a motivating or explanatory principle behind the problem while adopting imaginative and flexible interim solutions to the problem as you currently see it.

To begin working on this kind of problem, use the following small strategy, which is the same as Micro-Strategy 12. If you feel that your situation is really incomprehensible and unstable, then a more useful strategy might be Strategy 8, "Intractable."

MICRO-STRATEGY: FINDING A PATTERN.
Fitting the pieces of a situation into a pattern requires both imagination and painstaking effort. It's a little like trying to put together a giant's jigsaw in the fog. Seeing the whole picture is difficult. The questions in this micro-strategy switch you back and forth between the tasks of pulling the pieces together and looking for different ways to view the whole.

1. Are there any odd coincidences?

2. Can you reduce the range of issues you are looking at? Can you find a focus?

3. Is there a common thread running through all the parts of this problem? That is, are all or many of the parts related in some way?

4. What hidden or unstated goals or directions might there be?

5. Might you find a pattern by altering your viewpoint or changing your expectations of the situation?

6. Can you tease out, identify, and tackle a central problem or group of problems?

7. Could somebody be misleading you? Accidentally? Deliberately?

8. What is the most prominent, intriguing, fruitful, or useful aspect of this situation? Can you use it to find a new angle?

9. Can you start at the end and work backwards? Can you turn the problem upside down?

10. Is there anything here that is so much a part of the accepted way of looking at things that it might not be considered an issue?

11. Are you bringing to this situation an inappropriate or unrealistic set of expectations concerning the outcome, your capabilities, or the behavior or attitudes of others?

12. Might you find a pattern by delving into the assumptions, beliefs, concepts, or values with which you are approaching this situation and life in general? Can you examine the context in which you are setting all this?

13. Can you see decisive patterns in growth or change rates and directions, in components or factors, or in their interrelationships?

14. What are the basic items, assumptions, beliefs, or concepts that you are dealing with?

15. What exactly do you mean by the terms you are using, by the viewpoints you are expressing, by the questions you are asking?

16. How could you restate your attitudes, assumptions, or ground rules to reveal any need for clarification, reformulation, or tidying up?

17. Which parts of this problem are objective or verifiable and which are subjective, based on values, taste, opinion, or attitude?

18. Could you look at this problem in a way that throws a different light on it? That is, could it be seen as part of another issue? Could the problem be viewed as a chance to straighten out a different problem? Maybe it's an opportunity in disguise.

If you now have a clearer perception of your problem, go to Section 6. If you are still puzzled, try the quick-reference index or use Strategy 8, "Intractable," or go to "HELP," Section 12.

2-5. The situation doesn't seem anything like what you first thought it was.

Sometimes a situation you thought you understood can begin to confuse you and make you want to reorient yourself and start afresh. This often happens in getting to know people or in feeling a way into a new situation. It can also happen whenever you allow an old strategy to run on and on without reviewing it to see if it is still appropriate. Since you don't know what is happening, things that you couldn't predict can occur and the situation get easily out of control. Because you thought you did know what was happening you are probably halfway through various plans and actions based on a set of attitudes and expectations. Having to start afresh will seem disruptive and naturally you will want to resist doing this. But you must rethink the situation. Perhaps some of your work can be salvaged.

Here is a small strategy to help you adjust to a changed situation. This strategy is the same as Micro-Strategy 25.

MICRO-STRATEGY: REORIENTING TO A NEW PERCEPTION OF A SITUATION.

This micro-strategy should help you to establish what is different now, and the changes you must make as a result.

1. What seem to be the components of this new situation?
2. Who is involved?
3. What new facts or information do you have?
4. How have relationships changed? What new interactions are there?
5. What functions are different?
6. How has the overall situation, framework, or system changed? How is the total thing different?
7. Has the relationship between the situation and the world around it changed?
8. How have the dynamics of the situation changed? What's going on now? What new patterns or rhythms are there?
9. What is required to psychologically reorient yourself? What must you adjust to?
10. What attitudes must change? In yourself? In others?
11. What opinions must change? In yourself? In others?
12. How will your wishes and objectives be modified?
13. What concepts, ideas, frameworks, functions, or interactions should be modified?
14. What actions that are now under way must change?
15. What planned actions must change?

16. What new work, actions, plans, or problems must you deal with?

17. Has your perception of the time available or the situation's duration changed?

18. Have any deadlines changed?

19. What new opportunities are there?

20. How might you take advantage of this?

Now you may wish to turn to Micro-Strategy 3, "Organizing to tackle a problem," or to Micro-Strategy 8, "Planning ahead."

If you have gained a clearer perception of your problem, go to Section 6. If you are still puzzled, try the quick-reference index or go to "HELP," Section 12.

2-6. You are overwhelmed by detail and need to consolidate. There's too much going on.

This happens to most of us at regular intervals. It can occur when you're attempting to do too much, that is, when the associated problems increase and expand the scope of the main problem, or when you deliberately move further afield and overload yourself. It can also happen if you keep on accumulating ideas, tasks, or data without stopping to review, to consolidate, to devise patterns, and to categorize details. Sometimes exceptions or uncontrolled events accumulate and overwhelm you. This can occur when you have no guiding plan to keep your actions and procedures in harmony. Allowing an old strategy to run on too long can also cause all kinds of difficulties as circumstances change.

Organizational problems will arise when you fail to list your priorities in advance. When new events or tasks appear, it will be difficult to decide where they should be placed in your schedule. The situation will worsen if you keep changing your priorities and taking on new projects. All this fruitless activity will make you increasingly dissatisfied and will bring you closer to the situations described in Section 2-7, "You are losing your grip," or even Section 3, "Things are really getting out of hand." It's best to head the trouble off before it gets serious.

So, get organized and stay organized. Set your priorities, make a plan, act upon it, and don't fail to keep it under review. To begin, use the following small strategy, which is the same as Micro-Strategy 3, or try Micro-Strategy 29, "Consolidating."

MICRO-STRATEGY: ORGANIZING TO TACKLE A PROBLEM.
Making a good start is half the battle. Disorder usually leads to chaos. Clarify how you are going to operate now before the action starts. You may not have time to recover later.

1. What are you trying to do? Where are you trying to go?
2. What are the crucial aspects of this situation? What are the critical points?
3. What will be your signs of success? How will you decide when you have resolved things?
4. Is there anything special or unusual about this situation? Must you be especially cautious? Or can you take advantage of the special or unusual aspects?
5. At what level or from what direction should this problem be approached?
6. What are your targets? How much time do you need? Have you set deadlines? What are your priorities? How soon do you want the situation resolved?
7. What is the least that *must* be done?
8. What is the most that *can* be done?
9. Can a core of difficulty be identified?
10. How complicated does this problem seem to be? How many components, divisions, or levels does it have?
11. Can this problem be broken down into sub-problems that can safely be dealt with individually? Or can the situation be split up into distinct categories, parts, or areas of difficulty? What are these?
12. What are your strengths? How could you use these to respond here?
13. Can you see one point that might be easier than any other to find out about, tackle, or control? Can you do something about this?
14. In how many different ways can you reach your objectives? Which one seems to be the best choice? Which satisfies most of your criteria?
15. Should you consider a smaller range of events, or start with a part of the problem?
16. Should you tackle a larger problem that contains, causes or lies behind the present problem?
17. Should you take this problem one step at a time and reduce it piece by piece?

18. What seem to be the chief points to decide about or wrestle with?

19. Which areas look as though they'll need the most time, the most energy?

20. Which parts must be kept in harmony with each other?

21. What would be the most effective arrangement of all these pieces?

22. Should you give this solution a trial run before you decide about it?

23. How will you check what progress you're making?

If you feel your course of action is now a little clearer, go to Section 6. If you feel that you really have a complex situation on your hands, use Micro-Strategy 26, "For a Complicated Situation," or Strategy 3, "Complex," to tackle it. If you are still puzzled, then consult the quick-reference index of difficulties and strategies or go to "HELP," Section 12.

2-7. You are losing your grip on the problem situation. You are floundering.

You will probably start to lose your grip as a result of not knowing where to begin on an obscure problem, or if your problem keeps changing shape, or if you are overwhelmed by detail. At this level the complexity of problem solving becomes apparent. The difficulties you are facing may have multiple causes, all compounding each other. You may be trying to do too much and feeling confused and pressured. Impatience sometimes precipitates the difficulties. So do personal circumstances, which can lower your resistance to stress or interfere with your ability to think clearly. Alternatively, things may just be happening at too rapid a pace to be dealt with by the ordinary methods. Too much change, too much novelty, too much happening at once or continuing without an end in sight can overtax a person's ability to cope. Uncertainty, insecurity, and anxiety can result, reducing further your effectiveness at a time when your ability to operate is most important.

If you are in this situation, and conditions are becoming severe, you should go straight to Section 3. If the situation is only fairly bad, use the following procedure. The first step is to try to relax and become calm. Maybe you'd like to look through

Section 8, "An Interlude for the Weary." Sometimes the first response is to avoid the situation in sheer self-defense. This is not bad if—and only if—it means that you can rest and then reattack your problems.

What is the source of your main feeling of distress? Look through the following list to find a cause and a remedy.

YOU'RE FLOUNDERING, CONFUSED, MUDDLED.

This is an uncomfortable situation to be in. There may be more than one cause. And these causes may be overlapping, especially when you first take a look at your position. The following list contains a series of symptoms you may be experiencing in your muddled state. After that list is a series of possible causes for these symptoms and some suggested courses of action. The reason that symptom and cause are not directly linked here is

that you probably have a combination of effects at work. Only when you start to think about symptoms and causes together may you be ready to decide what kind of action appeals to you most. Work your way through the symptom list first, to figure out where you are. Then go through the list of causes and see how you feel about those. If none of these advances you in any way, try cause 5 in the list, and follow the advice given there.

SYMPTOMS.

1. You don't know how to assess your priorities, or they seem to switch around, or you can't choose priorities.
2. You can't identify problems to focus on, or it all looks equally confusing, important, or unimportant.
3. You can't decide what your objectives ought to be, or keep changing them, or haven't thought about them.
4. You keep being distracted. You're not absorbed by any of your tasks so you flit from one to the other looking for interest.
5. You're jumping from one thing to another in a panicky attempt to do everything at once, and not getting anywhere.

CAUSES.

1. Maybe it's not that you can't choose among your present alternatives, but that you need to search for a better alternative. Maybe you are bored or not sufficiently challenged. Perhaps you should look more closely at what you want to do.
2. Maybe you are viewing the situation at the wrong level, in too much detail, and missing the forest for the trees. Take a broader perspective. Look at things in the long term. Don't focus so closely. Perhaps a larger pattern or higher goal could help you to sort things out.
3. Maybe you are worrying unnecessarily. Perhaps all these things will take care of themselves and are not worth worrying about. How important will the problem be this time next year?
4. Perhaps these symptoms show a deeper problem, and

you should direct your effort and energies to thinking about this basic cause.

5. Maybe you're changing direction too often. Perhaps what you need is to focus on one thing for a long enough period to stabilize yourself. Then you might be able to find a different perspective. If this is the case, pick one of your problems and get on with it. Concentrate. Complete it.

6. Maybe you're putting together something new, working in the throes of creative composition where things float around in a muddle for a while and then suddenly crystallize into a new viewpoint, a new pattern, a new idea. Here, disorientation is normal. Relax and let the ideas run around for a while, between your efforts to pull it all together.

Now that you've worked through these symptoms and causes, look at the following sections for more specific symptoms and advice.

YOU FEEL UNMOTIVATED, JADED. MORALE IS SLIPPING.
Possible actions: Try one or more of the following to give yourself a boost.

—Talk over your difficulties with someone in an attempt to gain a different perspective on things.

—Take a break. Do something different to reinvigorate yourself. Even work on a problem in a different area.

—Or, just take a rest.

EVENTS ARE MOVING TOO FAST. TOO MANY THINGS ARE ASKING FOR ATTENTION.
Possible actions:

—Cut down to essentials, to what is required for survival, in order to reduce stress (see also Micro-Strategy 23). After a little recuperation at an easier pace your capacity should increase again. But take care to identify key tasks and make these your priority. Don't fuss with details at this point. Also try to avoid final decisions, or, decisions that don't include contingency plans in case the action backfires. Try to pick a pattern out of the confusion of events. Try to find a course of action that will solve more than one problem at a time. Make time to back off from the hectic bustle in order to detect such patterns and make such plans (see also Micro-Strategy 12).

YOU'RE UNABLE TO ORGANIZE, OR UNABLE TO STAY ORGANIZED FOR LONG.
Possible actions:
 —Plan a clear course of action. Don't be frustrated by the inevitable changes that any plan undergoes once it is applied. Keep your objectives clear, and relate actions and changes to your goals. You may wish to use Micro-Strategy 3 to get organized. Once you are under way, Micro-Strategy 22 could help you to stay on track.

YOUR OBJECTIVES ARE CONFUSED, VAGUE, OR CONTRADICTORY.
Possible actions:
 —Sort out the fuzziness and contradictions. Then delineate values, objectives, priorities, tasks, and requirements. For help with setting objectives, turn to Micro-Strategy 2.

IT'S ALL GETTING WORSE.
 —Go to Section 3.

After you've taken action, try answering the following questions to see if you have a clearer view of the situation.
 —Do you know what decisions you have to make?
 —Do you know what risks or uncertainties are involved in those decisions?
 —Do you know what different courses of action you may be able to take?
If you have answered these questions to your own satisfaction and feel you have a better grasp of your problem, go to Section 6, or return to the strategy you were using, or adjust your strategy to your new view of the situation, using the methods described in Section 15. If you have had trouble with the preceding questions, try Micro-Strategy 5 or 28, for help in defining your problem better.

Things Are Really Getting out of Hand

When you have a desperate feeling that life is something that happens *to* you, and that you have little control over events, then the situation is getting out of hand. You can become frustrated, anxious, hostile, or depressed and be tempted to take action of any kind just to demonstrate that you can be responsible. Under these circumstances, actions are often destructive and attention seeking. Sometimes the frustration is expressed in a self-destructive way, in withdrawal into inaction and feelings of inadequacy.

This kind of desperation comes about for various reasons. One cause is sheer overload. Events may be moving too fast. You may be trying to do too much, and feeling uncertain, confused, and pressured. Desperation can also develop when one of your major goals is being thwarted. Interference like this can make you feel threatened in a fundamental way. Meanwhile, life's ordinary problems continue, conspiring with this special situation to give you no peace. Impatience is sometimes a factor in this case. Often, time is required for a situation to evolve to fruition. In personal relationships, for instance, patience and care are needed to allow a relationship to grow at its own pace.

Perhaps you have made what seemed to be the best decision in the circumstances but now significant changes have altered the situation, or the situation continues to be uncertain and you begin to doubt the wisdom of your decision. Your doubts are becoming serious and you are encountering difficulties. Discouragement and fatigue from trying too hard and too long in the wrong directions can often contribute to this sense of things getting out of hand.

A first step in dealing with these conditions is, wherever possible, to back off. Get some rest. Engage in a calming activity. Be with friends. Or try reading through Section 8, "An Interlude for the Weary." Do something to break the obsession with the problem, something that could change your pace and viewpoint and help you to recuperate. Then try again, but more imaginatively, with an attempt to get things into perspective.

One way to gain a more balanced perspective is to look at your situation and focus on what is causing your distress. The following questions are designed to start you looking at your involvement in the problem. Take the questions seriously. Give some thought to them. They may help you to uncover the key to all kinds of other difficulties, too.

1. How are you responding to the situation? What sorts of things are you doing? How do you feel about it?

2. Is your response out of proportion to what triggered it? Is this an emotional reaction that is typical of you? Does your response involve a deeper emotional issue? What does this tell you?

3. Is the cause of your response an excuse, perhaps cleverly rationalized, for unloading frustrations from another area, from long-buried past events, for instance, or some other nonimmediate source? Can you pin down the real cause?

4. Are you failing to schedule and organize yourself properly so that your disorder is frustrating you and preventing you from achieving your first priorities? Are you frittering away your resources in short-term gains, in picking out the easy bits?

5. Can you pull out any central trends or patterns? How about your own behavior? Are you, or events, repeating a familiar pattern? If so, why? What is at the bottom of it?

These questions call for some pretty honest self-assessment, and could mean bad news for your self-esteem in the short term, but could also mean greater strength and self-respect in the long term. For example, you may discover that you are continually putting yourself down, rejecting yourself for every little failure, never giving yourself a chance because of this destructive self-criticism, and even wanting to fail as a subconscious self-fulfilling prophecy. To recognize this process, by yourself, through friends, or through counseling, and to rectify it takes a great investment of effort over a long period of time. The effort is valuable, though, because ultimately it can make you feel that you are a worthwhile person in your own right, and enable you to move with less fear and more confidence.

If you are in the mood to look more closely at how you might be a part of this problem, see if you can find yourself in some of the characteristics given below. If you do recognize yourself, examine how your involvement is linked to your present situation. This may help you to decide where the problem really lies.

—You set your goals too low; you're not challenged.

—You set your goals too high; you're always unfulfilled.

—You don't set goals; you're aimless.

—You don't look far enough afield. You restrict your life's inputs, confining yourself to your specialty. You don't get the stimulation of diversity.

—You don't take full responsibility for your actions. You leave decisions to someone else, ignore the consequences of your actions. You fail to take the initiative or to take control of your life. You take refuge in blaming others, blaming events, blaming luck and fate.

—You underrate yourself, ignoring your good points. You don't have the courage of your convictions. You fear failure, interpreting it as life rejecting you and proving that you are no good.

—You avoid making decisions, procrastinate, and hope for the best. You're afraid to act on your decisions; you don't follow through. You start off with enthusiasm, get bored, and keep changing direction.

—You dissipate your effort in a disorganization of detail, trivia, or irrelevance.

In your dealings with others:

—Do you constantly put people down?

—Do you criticize and never praise?

—Do you never make people feel appreciated?

—Do you keep people in the dark, denying them the information and feedback that they need or could benefit from?

—Do you fail to listen?

Many of these tendencies are traceable to negative feelings

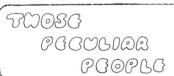

about yourself, which surface in your dealings with others.

These questions may help you to begin looking at yourself realistically. But *don't* make the mistake of listing all your failings. First make a list of your good points. Everyone has several important good points, though the person may never give himself a chance or may neutralize the good points. Keep your good points in mind when you consider these questions, and think of how these good points could be liberated!

If you cannot handle such probings at this time, at least make a careful attempt to clarify your present position and to list the difficulties and examine them one at a time. You can do this by using the following procedure. It will give you a means of bringing things sufficiently under control to consider some of the more specific remedies offered in Section 2.

Try to avoid any tendency to focus narrowly or exclusively on a small section of your life or a small section of time. You should place your worries in their broad context and in a large time scale to gain proper perspective, even though you may want to concentrate *action* on narrower concerns and single step-by-step tasks.

One other perspective-gaining approach is to ask this question: "How can I turn these troubles to my advantage? How can I turn all this into an opportunity?" This question might help to redirect your thoughts into more positive channels. Another method is contained in Micro-Strategy 10, "Seeking a change of perspective."

Let us look at ways of organizing a list of difficulties.

1. What events occurring in the short term must you deal with?

2. What are the things that you know you must do? Make a list of these tasks.

3. What is going wrong for you? What problems do you have *now* and what problems do you think you are *going* to have?

4. And, just to keep your spirits up, what is going right for you? How can you benefit more from this?

5. Which areas look as though they'll need the most time, the most energy?

6. Which activities need careful scheduling? What is the best scheduling of these?

7. Which activities are the most uncertain or raise the most questions?

8. Which parts will have the greatest impact if they succeed? If they fail? If they are delayed, disorganized, rearranged?

9. Which parts could give each other support? Can this mutual benefit be arranged?

10. What are your targets? How much time do you need? Have you set deadlines?

11. How are these detailed actions related to your larger objectives?

12. What activities are required for you to achieve your objectives? Or, what intermediate goals must you reach, and what activities do these goals require?

Now try to arrange your tasks in priority sequence as shown:

1. High priority—difficult
2. High priority—easy
3. Low priority
4. Fuzzy/unknown

Start to work on these. To do this you can use other sections of this book for guidance, for example, the quick-reference index of strategies and difficulties at the end of the book.

If you can't concentrate fully, get the easier high-priority tasks out of the way. Success in getting small things done gives a kind of boost, and also reduces mental clutter. When you're feeling better, work on the harder high-priority tasks. Pick one task and concentrate on it. Don't flutter around. Every day, take a look over the fuzzy tasks and try to see new angles. Try to resolve some of the confusion, but don't exhaust yourself on it.

Gradually the ordered approach should help to restore confidence. However, part of staying on top in such situations is to keep your eyes open and to think ahead. Your priorities may need to be changed at some point. So try to stay organized. Keep your lists of tasks up to date and in order of priority. Then you'll always be putting your best possible effort into the most important areas. Continual change in a situation affects decision making. Do all the work required to reach a decision and make the plans necessary to implement that decision. In addition, continue to gather information and keep an eye on things. Delay actually making the decision and committing resources until the last reasonable moment.

One of the hardest things to do when you are faced with a long-term problem of uncertain outcome is to maintain courage. Things could turn against you. You might not succeed. It's difficult to keep from doubting your direction and vacillating. And it's hard to handle the usual little problems that still go on alongside this large and enduring conflict. There's a temptation to throw in everything and relax into the illusion of a more secure, more easily attainable possibility.

One way of thinking about the problem is to remind yourself that when you began working on it you felt that you really wanted to resolve it. If your goal had already been achieved, would you want to give it up? Aren't the difficulties you're having to face to achieve what you want the only genuine obstacle? Then, your endurance is a part of the problem. Don't rationalize by saying, "Oh, maybe this isn't what I wanted after all." Don't try to back out. You still want it, so keep going. Take the situation day by day, or even hour by hour, if you must. Just keep on, do your best, and don't give in. The effort may exhaust you but you'll be stronger and more experienced afterwards. If you quit now, you'll have less strength and courage the next time around.

Then consider this question: Is there *more* that you can do to make things better? It may sound crazy, but when you feel most desperate, taxing your imagination by seeking new ways to get around the difficulty can help you to feel more positive.

Try not to worry if you keep failing. Failure can be a good way to learn and test yourself. It's a means to the kind of growth that eventually leads to success.

To avoid such distressing situations, or to reduce their frequency and severity, take the time to develop your skills of problem management and crisis handling. Try to predict and avoid difficulties by planning. Learn to generate flexible and superior solutions by practicing imagination and analytical judgment. In daily life, take more care with your problem solving and decision making. The skills and the confidence this process provides will then be at your command when you really need them.

Now you may wish to move on to some of the descriptions of difficulties in Section 2 for more specific advice. Or you may think you have a clear enough picture of your position to go to Section 6 and pick a problem-solving strategy. Alternatively, if you think your situation is best described as *intractable*, that is, not easily managed or manipulated, incomprehensible, unstable, rapidly changing in shape and activity, try Strategy 8.

Some General Remarks on Problem Solving

If you do not wish to read some general remarks on problem solving and strategies, skip to Section 6 to continue working on your problem.

As in the cartoon opposite, so in actual problem solving. We can question our way to clarity, and on to innovative and practical solutions. Searching, exploring, and puzzling are essential activities for solving problems. Hence, questioning is the basic method used in this book. The first question arises when we encounter or suspect a problem: What is going on here? Asking this question is the initial stage in the process of dealing with a difficulty. Here is a brief outline of the phases of problem solving, showing what stages follow this initial one.

Problem recognition—sensing a problem and gaining first impressions of it.

Planning—choosing an approach to take with the difficulty.

Problem definition—clarifying the nature, size, and shape of the problem.

Idea generation—using imagination to devise various focal ideas for solutions to the problem.

Solution building—elaborating the ideas of the previous stage into full-blown possible solutions to the difficulties.

Solution assessment—analyzing the alternative solutions and choosing one.

Approach assessment—examining what was done and why, and noting ways to benefit from this for the future.

Although this process may seem straightforward, in operation it may not be so orderly. As we work through a problem and all the things connected with it, we often move in cycles, not exactly going around in circles, but making successive attempts, mulling the situation over and returning to start again from a better vantage point, knowing our way around a little better.

Problem exploration often works hierarchically, too, following a pattern that's like the branching roots of a tree. We pull out the pieces of a problem and deal with these smaller parts, thus reducing the overall problem to more manageable chunks. This is very much like moving from a large root down to the smaller roots. Then sometimes we see that things are more complicated than we first thought, and we break up these chunks into even smaller pieces, finding problems within problems within problems. When we've solved the pieces we try to put this jigsaw of little solutions back together. Sometimes the resultant shape is different from what we expected and puts the issue in a startling new perspective, setting us off on a new problem-solving cycle.

Thus, it may be oversimplifying to say merely that we work our way through the basic problem-solving stages. Something else might be necessary to tie together all the branches, to link the cycles, and to accommodate any disruptions. To cover all the parts involved, it is helpful to have access to a problem-solving strategy that sequences and balances the different phases of problem solving to fit the requirements of the current problem. Strategies like this are included in this book.

In organizing the problem-solving effort, we must balance imagination with judgment, and innovative ideas with close analysis. This balance will change from stage to stage. For example, the idea-generation phase requires lots of imagination and little analysis. Solution assessment demands critical investigation, with some imaginative searching for loopholes. Problem definition needs an equal blend of both kinds of thinking.

As tacticians of problem solving we must perform this balancing act while weaving our way through the turbulence of daily life. We must assign the appropriate amount of effort to each stage and organize the stages into cycles to match the difficulties we are tackling. The results of weaving this coordinated and responsive problem-solving plan should be the discovery of a new pattern in the complex events around us, and eventually, an innovative and effective resolution of our difficulties.

Assembling action plans to deal with life's surprises and challenges is a central activity in our lives. It is a complex skill that involves selecting, planning, executing, and monitoring of the problem-solving procedure amidst the changes of everyday life. The skill takes some practice. This book offers help by providing ready-made strategies composed of checklists of questions and suggestions for action to guide you in your balancing and weaving activity.

These strategies are intended to help you make the compromise between speed and thoughtfulness—another of life's knife-edge balances. To cope with everyday life successfully, we must deal with problems quickly and effectively. Speed usually comes through practice on familiar situations, using known

skills and procedures. Because each problem is different, we must also ponder carefully each unique situation to determine the best course of action. This requires time.

The strategies are designed to move you quickly into action. They are also arranged and balanced to provide thorough coverage, to help you avoid thoughtfully analyzed but ponderously slow plans and speedy but ill-considered actions. They vary in specificity, eliminating the need to start from basics every time a new problem turns up. Each strategy has a framework general enough to be applicable to a range of similar problems. At the same time, the questions are specific enough to permit a problem to be tackled at once, with confidence. Strategies for handling both large and small problems are included, providing ways to approach a problem one piece at a time or as a complete package.

To begin selecting a strategy, work through the short set of questions in Section 6. These questions are designed to help you figure out what kind of difficulties you are facing. After deciding whether you have a large-scale or a small-scale problem, turn to one of the two sections recommended to examine the situation further.

For small-scale problems, you have the choice of taking things a step at a time, or in a single procedure. For the one-step-at-a-time approach, in Section 10, there are twelve stages and twenty-nine micro-strategies from which to choose. For the complete-package approach given in Section 11, six procedures are offered.

For large-scale problems, a set of eight strategies is provided. The procedures in these strategies are slanted to provide support in principal areas of problem situations. The strategies con-

sist of blocks of questions. Their structure and sequence are designed to guide your thinking and activity in solving the problem. The questions should not constrain your thinking process because they are open-ended and encourage exploration and further questioning. If you ever do feel confined, you can use the "HELP" section to restructure your approach. The strategies are intended to stimulate thought rather than restrict it or elicit one-word answers. For an example of how these questions work, turn to Section 5, a story called "Is the Dam Dangerous?"

As we have noted, the questions in the strategies are generalized to apply to any problem of a given class. Whether your concern is politics, biology, shipping, or personal relationships, whether you are coping with a complex problem or a fuzzy one, whether you are looking for a new idea or just trying to get organized, some activities and answers are basic. The questions will guide you.

Use the "HELP" section (Section 12) if you become confused, overwhelmed, or lost, or if you wish to review your position. You may find your problem situation changing, or you may change your mind about the kind of strategy you think is most suitable. You may become confused by the book's procedure or your approach. In all these cases, the "HELP" section can assist you.

The best explanation of a technique is found by using it and seeing what happens. So get into the system and get the feel of it as you start to come to grips with your problem.

Let's sum up the basic problem-solving procedure you will be following as you move through the book:

1. Make a first exploration of your difficulty.
2. Select a strategy or micro-strategy.
3. Employ the strategy.
4. Monitor it for adequacy as you work on your problem.
5. Modify it if you discover that the situation has changed or is different from what you thought it was and requires a new strategy, or if you find that you have picked the wrong strategy for the situation.

It is usually necessary to make repeated attempts on problems, so if you pass through this procedure a few times don't be concerned. For a story about the difficulties of pinning a

problem down, turn to Section 16, "Getting to the Root of it." At any point in your problem solving you may suddenly see it all from a different viewpoint and want to reorganize the problem situation, or some of the sub-problems, and start a new cycle based on the new insights or circumstances. Practical, effective solutions are what is important. If your problem keeps shifting around and changing shape as you look at it from new vantage points, keep in mind your overall objectives and values, and be patient with yourself.

Is the Dam Dangerous? An Example of Questions in Action

The purpose of this short story is to illustrate two micro-strategies in action. Interwoven through the narrative are the questions of, or the intent of, or the answers to the questions of, Micro-Strategy 1, "Taking a first look," and Micro-Strategy 12, "Finding a pattern." Through their explorations, the characters of the story uncover more than they had expected. They then search for a pattern in the puzzling information they have gathered. The story is designed to demonstrate that problems change shape as you work on them and that strategies must be used with awareness and flexibility.

The story.
It was a sunny day in Manzanita County. Springer was sitting on a rock beside a eucalyptus tree as Furry came scurrying along.
  "Hi, Furry," called Springer. "Where are you going?"
  "I'm going to find out about Greymist Dam."
  "What about it?"
  "There's a crack in it."
  "A crack! Is it serious?"
  "I don't know. It's leaking a million gallons a day."
  "That sounds serious," said Springer in alarm.
  "Well, I don't know whether a million gallons is serious or not. I don't know how to judge, but I aim to find out. Don't forget that other dam that collapsed three years ago near Woodland."
  "So what are you going to do?"
  "I'm going to get all the information I can and see what's

really involved," replied Furry. "First, I'm going to talk to the dam people. See you later."

Furry bustled off in the direction of the dam. In the meantime Springer thought about where else they might find information on the possible dangers of a cracked dam.

I guess if Furry's going to talk to the dam spokesperson, he'll probably also talk to some of the people who work there and get their opinions, she thought. Now, what could *I* do? I could talk to the state's emergency planners. Maybe they have criteria for when to start evacuation or some other kind of plan. I should also look up the reports on the collapse of the other dam. Maybe talk to the newspaper people, too. Then there's the construction company that built the dam. But I guess they'd give

SPRINGER ASKS FURRY WHERE HE'S GOING

me the bright side of everything. Hmmm. Ah, maybe if I found some people who were flooded out in the dam collapse, they'd have kept some information reports, and maybe done some research of their own.

She continued to ponder as she sat, sunning herself on her rock. Later, Furry stopped by with what he'd been able to find out.

"So, what's the story, Furry?"

"Oh, everybody seems to think it's not a problem. They say it's not uncommon for dams to leak. Anyway, this one is made of concrete, and the one that collapsed was made of earth fill."

"But this dam is much bigger than the other one."

"I know. This one is 550 feet high. The other one was 200. They said that the cracks are caused by temperature stresses. Something to do with the concrete curing."

"Did you ask them what might happen next? What if this dam collapses?"

"They keep saying it won't collapse, so they never answered my questions about what would happen if it did. But there's a 40-mile lake behind the dam with 500 billion gallons of water in it. Where would that go?"

"What are they going to do?"

"They're talking about lowering a huge vinyl curtain down the reservoir side of the dam. They say the water pressure would force the plastic into the crack and seal it."

"Is that the only way to do it?"

"Well, one person said that they could isolate the cracked section somehow and do a thorough job of mending it. But then they'd have to let a lot of water out of the reservoir and it would cost a lot of money to do it. Manzanita County would have to make arrangements to get water from somewhere else for a while, too."

"That affects what they say about the danger? Cost and inconvenience influence their opinions of safety?"

"Maybe so."

Springer told Furry about her ideas for getting more information.

"We should also go down to the public library," added Furry.

THOSE PECULIAR PEOPLE

WHAT'S THE MATTER WITH YOU?

OH, I BOUGHT ONE OF THOSE PLANNING SUPPORT ROBOTS

YOU MEAN THE KIND THAT HELPS WITH LONG RANGE PLANNING?

YES

ISN'T THAT A GOOD THING?

I THOUGHT SO, BUT IT STARTED TALKING ABOUT DYNAMIC AND FLEXIBLE OBJECTIVES FOR PLANNING IN A CHANGING SOCIETY....

.... THEN IT LOOKED AT MY PLANS

SO?

IT SAID I WASN'T DYNAMIC OR FLEXIBLE AND IT FIRED ME

"They have newspapers on microfilm. We could look up all about the old dam. The catalog would show if any books had been written about dam safety and design. We should investigate the history of all this."

"And the special reference works, abstracts, or guides to periodical literature might point us to articles and other sources of information. Then we could see what other people do."

"Let's go."

They hurried down to the library. A reference librarian directed them to some material on dam safety measures.

"Hey, look at this," exclaimed Springer after a moment. "In Sage County they have inundation maps."

"What are they?"

"They're maps showing what would be flooded if the dam fell down. Do we have those?"

"I don't know," Furry said. "We'd better ask."

"The law requires that they be available to the public. It also requires that Sage County have an emergency plan for dealing with a collapse. We should find out what *we're* supposed to have."

More research uncovered the fact that Manzanita County was under the same legal obligations as Sage County. Another ten minutes revealed that no inundation maps were available. Springer and Furry couldn't find any information about emergency plans. Their research did began to acquaint them with the complexities of water supply politics, with dam design, and with other states' emergency measures, compliance programs, disaster coordination, and advanced warning systems.

They decided to go down to the city engineer's office. Here they discovered another side to the question.

"It would cost a few million," reflected Big Joe Kress, the city's chief engineer, in response to Furry's question about fixing the dam. "Old Silvertwist wouldn't like that."

"Who?"

"Colonel Silvertwist. He owns the company that built Greymist Dam. He wants to build a big new subdivision in the northeast of the county. If he has to mend the dam he won't be able to start the subdivision."

"It wouldn't mean that much of a delay, would it?"

"Too long for old Silvertwist. He's been pulling together capital to build ever since the old dam collapsed. He built that one too, you know."

"Well, why aren't there any inundation maps?" asked Springer.

"The dam went over the budget. They couldn't afford to supply the maps. They had to cut costs somewhere, so that was what was cut."

"But isn't the state responsible for the maps, not the construction company?"

Big Joe Kress's rambling response didn't exactly answer the question. Furry and Springer thanked the engineer and went home to think about their findings.

Springer said, "Seems as though everyone is downplaying the danger because it would be difficult and expensive to fix the dam. I'll bet Silvertwist's company is deliberately playing it down. They've decided that it isn't serious because otherwise it would be so expensive."

"Yes, but there are other people involved in this and it would cost an awful lot more if the dam did collapse."

"But the insurance companies would pay, not the construction company."

"Now hold it a minute. The insurance companies, eh? I wonder what *they* would have to say."

"I wonder who insures the dam."

"Let's see if we can find out."

In the business section of the library a talk with the reference librarian, a phone call or two, and perusal of another document led to an interview with the South Manzanita Insurance Company.

The insurance company insisted that the state was responsible for producing inundation maps and emergency plans. "We have put some pressure on the government to get this done, but the proposals get shunted from committee to committee. We paid out last time, you know. I don't understand why old Silvertwist doesn't put on more pressure. His big subdivision plans got held up last time when we paid out all those damages."

"Silvertwist owns this insurance company?" exclaimed Springer.

"Oh, yes. I thought you knew that."

"We never even thought to check," said Springer, embarrassed.

After leaving the insurance company, Springer turned to
Furry and said a little ruefully, "I guess my Silvertwist conspir-
acy idea gets knocked on the head. Silvertwist would be caught
both ways. To fix the dam costs a lot. To have it fail costs even
more. So it doesn't look as though it's a plot by Silvertwist to
avoid paying. It would be in his interests to *fix* the dam if it's
dangerous. Maybe he assumes it isn't."

"Maybe *he's* getting bad information. Maybe someone is
leading someone astray for some reason."

"How would we get to the bottom of that?"

"Perhaps we could talk to Big Joe Kress again, and see some
of the people at the dam to find out how safety information is
coordinated."

Big Joe Kress greeted the two self-appointed detectives with
some amusement. They made a break in the usual rhythm of
his day. In response to their questions about how the dam's
condition was reported he said, "They send monthly reports on
dam functioning, water level changes, reserves predictions, and
so on, including any maintenance reports."

"No specific recommendations sections?"

"No, the person reading the report is supposed to pick up on
any problems."

"Are the reports looked at regularly?"

"We have a little office that pulls out the water supply statis-
tics to see how the city's water planning should be done. Then
the reports are passed on to Mr. Gorm, who reads them
through, if he has time."

"So danger warnings could be missed, like this crack business?"

"They could."

"It's really the information system that's at fault?"

"Well, perhaps it's the decision-making system too. Or
rather, a combination of the decision-making and information
systems—the bureaucratic system."

"If the information gatherers don't know what decisions are
going to be made, how do they know what information to collect? And if they don't have any emergency planning set up,

they don't know what constitutes the beginning of an emergency, or what would lead to the decision that there is an emergency."

"Funny how one problem leads to another," mumbled Furry.

Big Joe Kress was becoming intrigued by the flaws in the information and decision-making systems. He said he would try to find out how it was all set up.

During the next couple of days, Springer and Furry talked to people who had been washed out in the first dam collapse, and asked around to see if anyone else was working on this problem. Then Big Joe Kress phoned. He told them he'd been checking into what information went where. "Come over and let's talk about it," he suggested.

Later, in his office, Big Joe laid out what he had so far. "Do you see any interesting coincidences?" he asked when he had finished.

"Not really," replied Springer. "Just a few points where the information doesn't go to the right people."

"That's right," said Big Joe.

"Why is that so interesting a coincidence?" puzzled Furry.

"Because of what happens at the gaps," said Joe, triumphantly. "The official channels system has a number of holes in it. There is an unofficial grapevine that gets around the notes. At each of those gaps there are people who lunch together, or play squash together, or meet socially."

"You've really been digging," said Springer.

Big Joe laughed. "I've always spent a lot of time walking around and talking to all kinds of people. That's how the unofficial grapevine idea came to mind as a possible common thread running through all this."

"You're saying that the information system works after all because of the unofficial grapevine?"

"Right. But there's a funny kink. I think I've spotted another interesting coincidence."

"What's that?"

Big Joe consulted his notes briefly. "Of the fourteen people in the unofficial grapevine whom I talked to, nine of them at some point in the conversation mentioned Silvertwist, either as someone they had contact with, or someone they deliberately discussed things with, including what is going on in this situation.

"Aha! Silvertwist is tied back into it again."

"Exactly."

"But what might his objectives be?" asked Springer.

"Well, at the moment my ideas are all speculation," said Big Joe. "But look at it this way. Information is important. So if someone can influence, or modify, or manipulate the information that passes between certain points, that person can to a greater or lesser extent control the system."

"You mean, even though Silvertwist doesn't make the decisions, if he can manipulate the information on which the decisions are based, he might just as well be making the decisions?"

BIG JOE KRESS CONSULTS HIS NOTES

"That's right. If he knows where the gaps are, he can feed across the gaps the kind of information he'd like to see received on the other side of the gaps."

"Hmmm," mused Furry. "So he can color it with his own emphases. He can omit or downplay certain things, and perhaps keep some people bypassed or short of information. That would give Silvertwist a lot of power."

"And mostly because nobody would be likely to think his behavior questionable. A few conversations here and there don't seem so out of the ordinary, unless you really start to examine what goes where, and how it goes there."

"Well," murmured Springer thoughtfully, "it's a nice hypothesis and it could explain all that we know so far. Everything fits neatly into place. But how do we know this theory is true? Is there anything we've missed? What if it were not true? Then what?"

"Ah," said Big Joe. "I see where you're headed. Why don't we see if we can find a reason why the theory might be just plain wrong?"

"Yes," said Springer. "The best way to test it is to try to shoot it down, to think up different theories, and try to find conflicting evidence. If the theory stands up to all that, maybe it could be the right answer."

"Oh, my," said Furry. "This has turned out to be more complicated than I thought when I first set out to see if the dam is safe. Now we have all these interwoven problems. How will we unravel it all? What will we do next?"

Well, what would you do next? What would you have done so far that Springer and Furry didn't do? Did they miss anything?

THOSE PECULIAR PEOPLE

What Kind of Situation Are You in?

In this section you can assemble a picture of the kind of problem you have before you. If you think your problem is fairly straightforward, it still pays to take a closer look to see if things really are so clearly structured and defined. To help you with this, every strategy includes a definition or diagnosis stage to ensure that the situation is clarified, and to give you a clearly documented starting point.

The questions that follow constitute the first step in making your picture clearer. They should help you to choose a suitable approach to your problems.

1. What do you know about this situation?
2. What can you quickly find out?
3. Are there several problems here? Are they tied together, or loosely linked?
4. Are there uncertainties? Are they serious?
5. Can you easily see what the basic issues are? Or will you have to dig for them?
6. Is the problem so difficult that you are going to have to spend most of your time figuring out what is going on?
7. Do you need an immediate action plan?
8. Is the problem primarily a matter of getting organized, of making plans and establishing priorities? If so, how or why?
9. Should you seek information, find out where everything fits, or weigh, sift, assess, test, diagnose? If so, how or why?
10. Should you invent something new, produce a new plan or idea? If so, what or why?

11. Are you trying to sort out a confused or distressing situation, to avoid some unpleasant possibilities, or to get out of difficult circumstances? If so, what situation or why?

12. Do you have much time to work on this problem? How long?

13. Are you under pressures that make it hard for you to work on your difficulties? If so, what pressures or why?

14. Are your objectives clear? What do you really want to get done?

If your problem is only vaguely formulated, as problems so often are, spend more time in the diagnosis and definition phase, and even treat defining your difficulty as a problem in its own right. Use one of the problem-definition micro-strategies listed in the index, or use Strategy 1 or 5. Do this to ensure that you think about what the problem really is, that you consider all supporting or conflicting information that seems relevant, and that you work these findings into a clear picture of the problem. Then you can decide among the various possibilities for action.

Think about the factors that appear to be involved in the problem, and the time available to you, allowing for your other difficulties. Doing this will help you to select an approach as you work through the following section on categorizing a problem. For an example of questions in action read the story in Section 5, in which two people use micro-strategies to work on a problem of public concern. For a story on the difficulties of pinning a problem down, read Section 16.

Categorizing your problem.
Before you place your problem in a category, remember that you can obscure fundamental issues and discourage yourself by taking an elaborate approach right at the start. Overkill can result in a bureaucratic nightmare of procedures that rapidly drains your energy in unproductive effort. Use a broad-brush method in the beginning, and elaborate later when you have a clearer idea of the problem's shape. If your problem is large or difficult, for example, you may wish to become acquainted with it by quickly thinking up some ideas, however naive, that you think might solve it, or parts of it and then assessing the ideas to see whether or not they are ill conceived. This process can quickly

bring to mind areas and issues that must be taken into account, and can start you thinking about boundaries and ramifications. In fact, starting backwards in this way can strengthen your grasp of your directions and objectives, and of the problem as a whole.

At this point, two routes are possible. If you have a small problem—a personal one, for example, that involves some first probes of large-scale philosophical, technological, or scientific problems—then go to Section 9. Even if you have a large organizational problem, you could take this small-scale route as a way of putting things in order before you tackle your problem. This shorter approach is also good for pressured situations.

If you have a problem that seems fairly large, and includes various complications or tough organizational, corporate, political, or management issues, read Section 7, which follows, for a large-scale approach.

Problem-Situation Analysis: A Large-Scale Approach

This section contains a list of problem-situation descriptions. Think over what you learned about your problem from Section 6. Then select the *principal* characteristic of your problem situation from the characteristics described in the list. Proceed to the strategy suggested in the paragraph following the description.

If your time is short, use only the questions in the strategy that are marked with an asterisk.

If you are subject to interruption, try the following procedure to avoid fragmentation. At intervals, make a note of ideas you are entertaining, important facts you have gleaned, tasks you have planned, and deadlines. The strategies are divided into segments to provide stopping points. Thus, if the interruptions are frequent or unpredictable, you have a position you can return to and your thoughts will not be lost. It would be a good idea to note down your current position at the end of each segment. Then, if you are distracted or disoriented, you will never be more than one segment away from where you were working.

The questions in the strategies may not always seem directly applicable to your situation. They are designed to direct your thoughts to particular areas and thus should stimulate you to think of the right questions or of more specific questions. The questions may also provoke thoughts about other areas to investigate and lines of inquiry to follow. Be judicious in deciding how far afield to go in pursuing these additional questions. Without care, you may lose track of the project or become overwhelmed with detail.

You can move back and forth among the strategies, if you wish, to get an idea of the kind you need. To do this, work quickly through the following list of characteristics, select a strategy, read through the introduction to your strategy, and look over its outline. See how this feels. Then return to the list of characteristics and reselect if you need to. You should have a better idea of what the characteristics imply.

Problem-situation descriptions.

1. *Straightforward.* No particular surprises or complications are expected. It's just a question of working your way through a relatively uncomplicated task, though this may require a fair amount of thought and effort. Try Strategy 1.

2. *Straightforward but pressured.* You have a straightforward problem as described in 1, but you are under pressure and may have to act sooner than you'd like. Try Strategy 2.

3. *Complex.* The problem has many parts or sub-problems that are interrelated or interacting in involved or changeable ways. The situation is quite intricate. Go to Strategy 3.

4. *Unpredictable.* The situation is uncertain and changeable. Both the surrounding circumstances and the events within the problem shift around in a manner that cannot be known in advance. "Unpredictable" differs from "intractable" (description 8) in that the unpredictability is confined to some areas of a situation that is not in itself a mass of thorny, inexplicable problems, as intractable situations are. If your circumstances seem intractable, then go to description 6 or 8. If they seem only unpredictable, try Strategy 4.

5. *Fuzzy.* The problem is hard to grasp, control, resolve. It is subtle, obscure, formless, confusing, difficult. A brain teaser. Try Strategy 5.

6. *Complex, unpredictable, and fuzzy.* This description combines the difficulties of descriptions 3, 4, and 5. To deal with this situation try Strategy 6. Or, look at descriptions 7 and 8 to see if they provide a better outline of your position.

7. *Crisis.* You are in an unstable, difficult situation of immediate impact as well as decisive consequences in its outcome. Use Strategy 7.

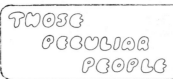

8. *Intractable.* You are in a situation that is not easily managed or manipulated, incomprehensible, unstable, rapidly changing in shape and activity. This description combines the worst aspects of descriptions 3, 4, and 5, and threatens some crises. To try to come to grips with this situation use Strategy 8.

At this point you may be feeling frustrated, thinking that it's not so much a question of problem solving, but of choosing among alternatives. If you feel this way and you need to move quickly, try Micro-Strategy 13. Before you do so, remember that bad decisions are made sometimes by inadequately defining and assessing the problem situation, and thereby producing too limited a range of possible actions. If you still do not want to make a full-scale problem-solving effort, you can use the tail end of a strategy in the following way:

Strategy 1: use part 5 onward.
Strategy 2: use part 5 onward.
Strategy 3: use part 12-1 onward.
Strategy 4: use part 7 onward.
Strategy 5: use part 6 onward.
Strategy 6: use part 6-2 onward.

Strategies 7 and 8 are not suitable for partial working.

When you have located your strategy, you're ready to start on your problem. If you run into difficulties at any point, go to Section 12, "HELP." This section is useful also if you want to take stock, reassess or modify your approach, or start from a better perspective, that is, if you want to review and rethink in any way.

So, describe your problem situation, select your strategy, and tackle your problem.

An Interlude for the Weary

"I'm sure this isn't the way home, Pepper," puffed Hoot as they struggled through the vegetation that was choking the gully they were climbing.

"Come on, Hoot," Pepper replied. "Just a little more effort."

"I think we're going the wrong way," said Hoot. "We're lost."

"No, we're not."

Pepper pushed on through the intertwined roots and wet, dripping leaves.

"We'll soon be out of this thick stuff," Pepper said. "Then we'll be able to see a bit more clearly."

"Why are we climbing?" Hoot asked. "I thought the way home was downhill."

Pepper sighed and turned to Hoot. "It is. But first we have to make sure we're going down the right hill. To do that we have to look out from a higher point."

"I'm tired," responded Hoot.

"OK, we'll rest for a while. The way home will still be there in half an hour."

They sat and rested. As they did so, the sun gradually crept out again and began to dry their damp clothing. The wet leaves started to dry out too. Small yellow butterflies came out to flit around, and the scents of sage and eucalyptus mingled in the air.

"Well, I'm feeling a lot more cheerful now," said Hoot after sitting peacefully for a while. "This little problem doesn't seem half so bad, even though we are lost."

Pepper grinned. "Maybe we're lost now. But we're not going to stay lost. Are we?"

"No, we're not." Hoot laughed. "OK, Pepper. You're right. Let's go uphill again."

Refreshed by their brief rest, they made good progress even though the vines and foliage seemed to get denser for a while.

"It's clearer ahead," called Pepper after an interval.

Soon they were scrambling over boulders and lichens toward a high point on the hill.

"There. Now we can see what's what," Pepper said as she looked around in all directions.

"Well, this gives us a better idea of what routes we might take," agreed Hoot.

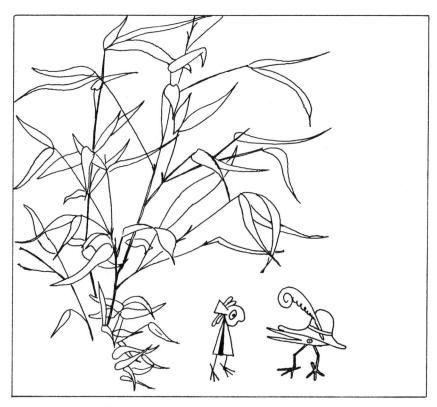

HOOT AND PEPPER REST A WHILE

They looked down from the top of the hill and after a while they determined which direction was home.

"Which route would be best?" wondered Pepper.

"The fastest route," said Hoot, pointing to the direct route.

"Hmmm. I'm not so sure."

"Yes, I suppose there are some tricky, rocky sections to negotiate. Oh, and there's a cliff to climb too," he continued.

Slowly Pepper looked all the way around. She nudged Hoot. "Look there," she said.

Hoot looked. "Well, it's a nice gentle trail," he said. "Looks as though it could be quite an interesting walk too. But it goes in the wrong direction."

Pepper smiled. "It only seems to. Look further ahead, Hoot."

Hoot did so. The trail wound gently around, and could be seen meandering past all the obstacles that the other trail presented. It looked as though they would be home more quickly if they followed the indirect trail.

"Come on, Hoot, let's go."

Revitalized, Hoot and Pepper set off for home and learned a great deal as their trail wound in and out of parts of the wood they'd never seen before.

As with Hoot and Pepper's solution to their problem, much of good problem management, that is, problem recognition, definition, and resolution, is a question of shifting perspectives. What seems hopeless or impossible from one viewpoint may suddenly seem relatively easy, and certainly less worrisome, when your viewpoint changes. Bearing this aspect of problem solving in mind can make you more confident, less pressured and worried, when you approach a new difficulty. It's hard not to be anxious and tense when faced with obstacles to fulfillment. Indeed, complacency in the face of difficulty often brings on a more serious situation. A little tension will provide motivation and ensure that you attend to your difficulties. But, take it too far, and you'll have incapacitating worry or panic.

Often a problem seems most hopeless and impossible just before it's solved. Maintaining your confidence that you can find a new perspective if you try will help to keep anxiety within bounds. If you are reading this, then you are alive today, and must have solved your problems so far in some fashion. With a little care and practice, you can do it still better in the future— a lot better.

Small-Scale Problems

At this point you may choose to tackle your problem one step at a time or all at once in one concentrated effort. If you want to take the situation stage by stage, go to Section 10. If you want to work on the whole problem using a complete strategy, go to Section 11. If you are concerned mainly with decision making, use Micro-Strategy 13. Remember to be careful, to be sure you're looking at the full range of options, and have a clear enough picture of the problem. Speedy decision making is admirable, but only if you're solving the right problem.

One Step at a Time

Look through the following list of stages and pick the one that seems closest to where you are with your problem. Proceed to the micro-strategy shown, to start work on your project. If there's a choice, take the first micro-strategy given. If you're having trouble getting started, try Micro-Strategy 1.

As a result of working on your problem with the micro-strategy, you may begin to see your problem situation differently and wish to return to Section 6 to choose a new way of tackling it. Or, you may want to consult an additional micro-strategy. The table of contents has a complete list of micro-strategies.

Stages.
1. First look: 1.
2. Setting objectives: 2.
3. Getting organized: 3.
4. Making a crisis plan: 6.
5. Exploring and diagnosing: 5, 4, 7, 11, 26, 27, 28.
6. Generating new ideas: 9, 10.
7. Forming plans or solutions: 14, 8, 13, 12, 23, 11.
8. Reviewing the problem: 15.
9. Reviewing the solution: 16, 17, 18.
10. Staying organized: 22, 21, 25, 29.
11. Implementing a solution: 19.
12. Reviewing your approach: 24.

Tackling a Small-Scale Problem as a Whole

Look through the descriptions that follow and decide which one best fits your picture of your problem. Then take the action indicated in the paragraph.

1. *Straightforward.* No surprises or complications are expected. It's just a question of working your way through a relatively uncomplicated task. Try Strategy 1, using only the questions marked with an asterisk.

2. *Crisis.* Things are falling apart and something must be done. Use Strategy 7.

3. *Pressured.* You have a straightforward problem, but you may be forced to take action sooner than you'd like. Go to Strategy 2 and use only the questions marked with an asterisk.

4. *Mainly planning.* If you are primarily interested in figuring out what action to take to achieve particular goals, try Micro-Strategy 8. If you just want to get organized, turn to Micro-Strategy 3.

5. *Complex.* There are many problems, all interlinked. The situation is quite intricate. Try Micro-Strategy 26.

6. *Unpredictable.* The circumstances are uncertain and changeable. Things may switch around on you a lot. Go to Micro-Strategy 27.

HELP

The monitoring and reassessment activities in this section are designed to help you out of whatever difficulty you are in. They offer guidance if you want to review or readjust. The step-by-step guide should help you through your puzzlement to a suitable course of action. If you wish to take advantage of this process, continue through this section. If you need a fast response and you know what your difficulty is, then consult the quick-reference index of difficulties and strategies at the end of the book. For a refresher on what problem solving is all about, read Section 4.

Breaking down your position.
Which of the following descriptions best expresses the position you are in?

1. *In difficulties.* You are confused and becoming distressed or pressured. Or you're in a crisis situation. Go to Section 13.

2. *Wanting to take stock.* You'd like to review your progress, the problem situation, or the appropriateness of your strategy. Go to Section 14.

3. *Wanting to change your approach.* You want to start over from scratch, or adjust an inadequate strategy. Go to Section 15.

In Difficulties

Let's look at your difficulties more closely. Which of the following descriptions most closely fits your situation?

1. *In crisis.* If you are caught up in a crisis situation go to the strategy for dealing with crisis, Strategy 7. Or, if you are really distressed, turn to Section 3.

2. *Crisis situation close at hand.* For a way of dealing with impending crisis, go to Micro-Strategy 23.

3. *Confused, I.* If you are confused about the problem situation, puzzled by the events, or losing your grip on the problem, turn to Section 2.

4. *Confused, II.* If you are confused about the strategy or approach you are using, or are becoming entangled in your procedure, continue reading in this section.

5. *Confused, III.* If you are confused about dealing with this problem-solving system read Section 4 for an explanation of the system. See also the flowchart in the introduction to the book.

6. *Distressed.* If you are becoming distressed and feel pressured, go to Section 3.

Feeling uncertain about your approach.
Situations tend to change as you work on them. When this happens, the approach you originally devised to deal with the difficulty may cease to be appropriate. In other instances, your interpretation of the situation may not be clear enough for you to tackle it correctly. In either case, your lack of the tools you need can send you down blind alleys, involve you in unproductive effort, and perhaps make you confused and disoriented. You keep wondering why you are floundering about.

It is normal for a problem to look different as you learn more about it. This is part of the understanding process that precedes the solution of your difficulties. Problem solvers tend to proceed in cycles. They diagnose a problem, try to solve it, find a better idea of what the problem is about, and then try to solve the clearer problem. Sometimes this process leads to the solution of a bigger problem than the one the problem solver started out with. These cycles should not be confused with aimless wandering in circles. *Think, test, and rethink* is a standard problem-solving procedure. The more difficult and changeable the problem situation, the more numerous the reinterpretations and restarts will be, as various aspects of the chaotic situation are pinned down. In a more stable problem situation, a more direct route to a solution can be taken.

If your strategy is unsuitable for the situation, you will have difficulty. If you use a loose and exploratory approach in a situation that demands careful coordination, tight scheduling, and optimization of numerous events or tasks, nothing will ever get done; confusion will reign. On the other hand, if the strategy consists of a highly structured timetable of actions in a fast-moving, unpredictable situation, a great deal of effort will be spent, producing only out-of-date results.

A strategy can produce poor results also if your thinking as you operate the strategy is unbalanced. Perhaps you are using too little judgment, and too much imagination. Perhaps you are being too critical and not sufficiently creative. Or perhaps you are using appropriate amounts of imagination and judgment, but you are not properly organized. Analysis and creativity must interlock in a way that's appropriate to the situation.

Looking at the need for balance in another way, you may be placing inappropriate emphasis on some parts of the problem-solving plan. You may not have paid enough attention to your objectives and so may be operating with unclear guidelines. You may not have devoted enough time to figuring out what the problem was before you started to solve it, and so may be cheerfully solving the wrong problem. You may have devised an interesting solution to the problem, but not have paid enough attention to the impact the new solution will have in some areas. Careful thought must be given not only to the im-

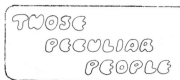

THOSE PECULIAR PEOPLE

SO WE PUT IN THIS NEW COMPUTERIZED MANAGEMENT SUPPORT SYSTEM

IT MAKES ALL THE ROUTINE DECISIONS

IT TAKES A LOT OF RESPONSIBILITY OFF THE MANAGERS, BUT THEY DON'T SEEM TO LIKE IT

DID YOU GIVE THEM RESPONSIBILITY FOR NON-ROUTINE DECISIONS IN PLACE OF WHAT YOU TOOK FROM THEM?

NO

THAT'S LIKE GROWING A PLANT AND NOT EXPECTING IT TO FLOWER

GULP

plications and ramifications of your actions, but also to how the new solution is going to be implemented—often another problem in itself. Make sure you have the emphasis right.

To pin down your interpretation of the situation so that you can modify your strategy appropriately, look at Micro-Strategy 7, "What's going wrong here?" or Micro-Strategy 15, "Reconsidering the problem situation." When you have found out what you need to do, go to Section 15 to exchange your strategy for a more suitable one.

Taking Stock

Decide which of the following statements most clearly describes your requirements and proceed as indicated.

1. You wish to review your progress to assess the organization and effectiveness of your work so far and the appropriateness of the strategy being used. Go to Section 14-1.

2. You wish to review the problem situation itself, to rethink, to reexamine. Go to Section 14-2.

14-1. Reviewing your progress.

Look the situation over by considering the questions that follow. These questions are similar to those contained in Micro-Strategy 24.

1. Are you achieving your overall objectives?

2. Have your actions had the required effects? If not, why did they fail? How much success did you have and why?

3. Does the reason for failure present you with any insights?

4. If your actions were a success, can you do still more?

5. Have your actions or their effects presented new opportunities? If so, what can you do to exploit these?

6. Were your actions really effective, or are appearances deceiving you?

7. Did something just happen or change? If so, will it affect the situation? Where does the event or change fit? What could be done about it?

8. Should you implement your crisis plan? Do you have a crisis plan? If not, use Micro-Strategy 6 to devise one.

9. Does the situation look as though it is changing or about to change?

10. Has the situation already changed in a manner that's hard to recognize? Is the situation different even though it seems the same?

11. Has the situation remained fundamentally the same despite apparent changes?

12. What would be a surprising way the situation could change?

13. Imagine that the situation, events, or participants are conspiring to surprise you. What would be your weakest spot? What might happen?

14. What could you do to be ready for this?

15. What else is going on? Is it significant? Can you connect the situation with these other things going on, either by discovering subtle links or by making an innovation?

16. If you can see anything that might go wrong, can you think of a way of handling it or preventing it?

17. Have you gained new perspectives? Does one of these viewpoints indicate that a new solution or new approach is possible?

18. Do any new problems need to be solved? If so, how will you organize this?

19. Should you reorganize or reschedule any part of the current effort? Should you change priorities, expand, contract?

20. Did you approach the problem in the most effective way? Did you take the best course of action?

21. Did you try to cut out activities that did not contribute directly to the overall objectives? Did you concentrate on the activities that did contribute?

22. Can you improve the way you tackle problems so that you can devise better solutions in the future?

If you are not satisfied with your results, one of the many possible reasons might be that you have not been using the correct strategy. If you think this might be the case, look at the following questions to determine what is wrong with your approach. These questions are also contained in Micro-Strategy 20.

1. Should you speed up or slow down?

2. Are you going into the problem in sufficient depth?

3. Are you dithering around? Could your work be more concentrated?

4. Are you working in the areas that look as though they'll provide the biggest effects or contributions?

5. Are you putting first things first?

6. Is anything you are doing, or contemplating doing, trivial or superficial?

7. How might you be running into difficulties? By attempting too much, by delaying, by avoiding difficulties? By being unrealistic; by oversimplifying; by taking action that is inappropriate to the day-to-day, personal, business, or political realities? By being uncoordinated, impractical, or overcomplicated?

8. Is there a more adventurous, more inspired, or bolder way of doing this?

9. Are you overdoing it? Is your approach too cumbersome or complicated?

10. Is anything slipping? Organization, motivation, timing, imagination, judgment, critical review?

11. Can you do less in any area?

12. Could a redirection of effort enable you to make more progress?

13. Do you need a boost for your spirits? Do you need your strength restored? Could friends help?

14. Are you taking on too much? Are you being erratic or panicking because of stress or sudden change?

15. Do you keep changing direction? If so, is it because you are losing your grip on the situation?

16. Are you keeping a clear overall view of the situation? Can you spot trouble before it arrives?

17. Have you been behaving flexibly, imaginatively, and coherently? Can you get a second opinion from someone?

18. Have you changed your view of the situation considerably? Must you now change your approach?

19. Is your approach really suitable? Are your techniques appropriate? Are you being too precise, or too slapdash?

20. Do you really need help in handling this situation?

21. Are you turning a blind eye to anything?

22. Are you in any way causing the difficulties you are faced with?

23. Can you see ways in which you might improve your problem-solving behavior?

Now perhaps you should look for an approach that accommodates the inadequacies you have discovered in your present strategy. Try Section 15, which contains ways both to modify and to start again from scratch.

14-2. Reviewing your problem.

To reexamine the problem situation, consider the following questions. They are the same questions as those contained in Micro-Strategy 15.

1. Could the situation be reorganized? Could you see it from different perspectives?

2. Do you have any information at hand that could show that the situation is not what it seems?

3. Is this problem worth solving? If so, what degree of effort seems appropriate?

4. Is there anything that is so much a part of the accepted way of looking at things that it might not be considered an issue?

5. Do you feel that you have grasped what is happening?

6. Do you have any misgivings about your information? If so, examine the uncertain area carefully. Does your examination lead to different interpretations?

7. Who could give you another outlook on the situation?

8. What other things could your interpretation of the situation imply or lead to? Can you find evidence for this? Does considering this question lead to new avenues of inquiry?

9. What can be inferred from this situation? What does it imply? What does the situation lead to?

10. How is this situation developing? What is its history? What could its future be? How many different ways could it develop in the future?

11. Does this raise deeper issues?

12. Are things actually more complicated than this, or simpler?

13. What is puzzling you?

14. Should you tackle a larger problem that contains, causes, or lies behind the present problem?

15. Are you trying to tease out the truth, or to construct what you would like to find?

16. How can you solve this problem most advantageously?

17. Is this situation part of a larger problem?

18. Do you have to look beyond the present range of events to find the causes, or the motivating or controlling forces?

19. What hidden or unstated goals or directions might there be?

20. Are you looking at the problem upside down?

Next, go to Section 6 to take whatever action now seems necessary.

Changing Your Approach

This section is composed of a list of conditions, followed by a list of remedies. The conditions cover various reasons why you might wish to modify the strategy you are using. The remedies tell you how to make the necessary changes.

Decide which of the following statements describes your requirements and proceed as directed.

1. *You want to start over from scratch.* Go to Section 6. Also consult the index of difficulties and strategies at the end of the book for ways to patch up or restore your situation.

2. *You want to adjust an inadequate strategy.* Read on.

Adjusting an inadequate strategy.

CONDITIONS.

Select your condition or conditions from the following descriptions. Then consult the paragraph bearing the same number in the remedies section.

1. The strategy is too long, but otherwise fits the situation.

2. It's too cumbersome, too involved. You really want something much shorter and to the point.

3. It's too short. You want more detail, something more elaborate and thorough.

4. The strategy ought to be more detailed in some places, less detailed in others.

5. You want something small, but more complete than the micro-strategies. You want a whole strategy, not just a procedure that tackles aspects of the problem.

6. Time has suddenly run short. You want to speed up.

7. The strategy isn't complete. It's basically sound but some bits are missing.

8. The problem has turned into an array of problems.

9. You need just the decision-making aspect of a strategy.

10. You want a more casual, less structured approach.

11. The emphasis is wrong. The strategy doesn't concentrate on the areas you need to work on, and overdoes it in areas you're less concerned with.

12. The strategy needs fine tuning. You want to modify it yourself.

13. The problem situation has changed, or you see it differently.

14. It's not the right strategy. It ought to be reconstructed.

15. The characteristics-selection method doesn't get you what you want.

If you are already well involved in the strategy that you wish to change, try using Micro-Strategy 29 to clarify your position.

REMEDIES.

1. Follow the most suitable procedure of these three:
—If you selected your strategy using Section 7, go now to Section 11.
—If you selected your strategy using Section 11, go now to Section 10.
—If you have been using all the questions in your strategy, now try using only the ones marked with an asterisk.

2. Turn to Section 10 and follow the step-by-step procedure for selecting micro-strategies. Micro-Strategy 8, "Planning ahead," and Micro-Strategy 3, "Getting organized," might be good selections.

3. Follow the most suitable procedure of these three:
—If you have been using a micro-strategy selected in Section 10, now try using the medium-sized approach offered in Section 11.
—If you have been using the medium-sized approach in Section 11, now try the full-sized approach in Section 7.
—If you have been using only the questions marked with an asterisk, now try using all the questions.

4. Omit from the strategy the sections, paragraphs, or questions that you don't want. Then, using the list of micro-strategies in the table of contents as a guide, take from selected micro-strategies a few questions to substitute for the overly detailed sections of the strategy you've been using, and questions that provide additional coverage for the areas that you find too thin. If you prefer to tailor your own strategies, consult the author's book, *Successful Problem Management*, which describes how this can be done.[1]

5. Consult Section 11, to find a small, complete strategy.

6. First, consolidate your position using Micro-Strategy 29. This micro-strategy should help you to clarify where you are. Then move to a shorter strategy by following one of the procedures listed in paragraph 1 or 2 in this section.

7. You can add to your strategy by attacking micro-strategies in some places. Select micro-strategies by using the table of contents.

8. When you are working on a large problem, various additional obstacles, difficulties, reviews, and sub-problems can turn up. It isn't always necessary to rework your strategy to accommodate these developments, especially if the strategy is a large one. Instead, pick a micro-strategy from the table of contents, work through it, and then return to your original strategy. In this situation you may find that after a while you are spending more time using these extra micro-strategies than you are using the original strategy. If, as a result, your approach becomes too cumbersome or confusing, it is time to simplify your approach and change to a more coherent strategy. Here are two choices to help you:

—Move to Strategy 3, "Complex," or to Strategy 6, "Complex, unpredictable, and fuzzy."

—Use Micro-Strategy 8, "Planning ahead," or Micro-Strategy 3, "Organizing to tackle a problem," to analyze and organize the array of problems.

9. Read the discussion of decision making that follows the problem-situation descriptions in Section 7, or go to Micro-

[1]Michael Sanderson, *Successful Problem Management* (New York: John Wiley & Sons, 1979).

Strategy 13, "Decision making and selecting from alternatives."

10. You may wish to proceed by selecting micro-strategies from the table of contents whenever you feel you need some structured help. Bear in mind, though, that with all problems it is necessary to move through a number of stages, no matter how casually. First, you must establish what you intend to do and why. Then, you must clearly define or analyze what your problem is. Next, you must use your imagination to generate ideas for possible solutions. The more ideas you consider the better. Then, you have to build the ideas into two or three workable solutions, specifying ways to put the solution into effect. Then, a period of critical analysis is required. During this time you should look for flaws in your solution, and repair them. Next, select the best solution and put it into effect. Once the solution is in effect, you must reexamine the whole situation objectively and consider what you see. More problems? For additional information on the problem-solving process, turn to Section 4.

11. Read the advice given in paragraph 4 in this section. Also reflect on the general problem-solving stages outlined in this section in paragraph 10.

12. Paragraph 10 in this section provides an outline of problem-solving stages required in any approach. Paragraphs 1 through 4 indicate procedures for increasing and decreasing the size and coverage of your strategy. For advice on how to construct strategies from scratch, see the author's book, *Successful Problem Management.*[2]

13. Follow the most suitable procedure of these three:

—Turn to Section 2-4, "The problem keeps changing shape," or Section 2-5, "The situation doesn't seem anything like what you first thought it was."

—Go to Micro-Strategy 25, "Reorienting to a new perception of a situation."

[2]Michael Sanderson, *Successful Problem Management* (New York: John Wiley & Sons, 1979).

—Return to Section 6 to try rebuilding your approach.

14. Return to Section 6.

15. Follow the most suitable procedure of these four:

—Use the paragraphs in this remedies section to modify your strategy until you think it's better.

—From the table of contents select micro-strategies to substitute for, or supplement, your strategy.

—Use the index of difficulties and strategies to find a wider range of pieces for your approach.

—Build your own strategies by using the author's book, *Successful Problem Management*, in combination with this book.[3]

---

[3]Michael Sanderson, *Successful Problem Management* (New York: John Wiley & Sons, 1979).

Getting to the Root of It: A Story of Steel Making

In the following story, some practical difficulties involved in problem definition and problem isolation are explored through the activities in a steel-making corporation. In the story, the characters show how difficult things can become when people blunder on with little feeling for a systematic approach. The events of the story demonstrate that systematic approaches must be used flexibly and with awareness if these approaches are to produce their intrinsic benefits and not make things worse.

The story.
"Now there's something I hadn't thought of," said Hoot as he and Pepper made their way along the catwalk. From their vantage point twenty feet up on the side of the steel-rolling mill, they were looking down on the twenty-ton yellow-orange steel ingot. Even at that height the heat from the glowing steel was making them uncomfortable. Involuntarily, they paused to watch for the hundredth time with fascination as the steel trundled toward the rollers. There came the loud crack of water turning explosively to vapor as the yellow ingot hit the water-running rollers and was squeezed a few inches flatter and longer. As the ingot passed through the rollers, an arm came out and prongs from the rolling bed pushed up to throw the ingot on its side. Then the rollers reversed and the ingot was squeezed back through. After being reduced in cross section, and increased in length, several times, the steel was passed on to a huge set of shears, to be chomped into shorter sections ready for reheating and rolling down to smaller sizes at the next roller station.

"What hadn't you thought of?" said Pepper, eventually, as they moved on.

"If we're going to put computer terminals around the plant to record the progress of various orders, the terminals are going to have to be able to withstand this heat."

"Or be located somewhere else, or be shielded, or insulated or something."

"All we need is another complication in this planning-and-progress-system proposal."

"Yeah. But it does underscore the idea that you've really got to get the feel of a problem at all levels if you want to cover all the angles."

"True, true," agreed Hoot. "It's a real waste of time to put into effect a badly thought-out solution."

"Some people do that because they claim there isn't time to look at every last detail. They say they can work out the bugs once it's under way."

"Well there's something to be said for that. Speed is vital. But there are two things wrong with that idea. First, thorough work and a good solution can be carried out in the same amount of time as an untidy solution can if you go about it systematically and imaginatively."

"That's right. You've got to be both things. Being systematic and unimaginative is just as useless as being imaginative and unsystematic."

"Yes, and working out the bugs afterwards isn't always so easy. First, it costs time and money, and second, you sometimes find things that just cannot be accommodated no matter how you bend and twist your solution. Then you're worse off than before you started."

"Well," sighed Pepper, "this planning and progress system is a real challenge. I'm looking forward to it."

They walked along the catwalk and down the staircase on the other side of the rolling mills and headed for the administrative offices.

"I wonder what surprises there'll be at the meeting today," Hoot ventured.

"There's usually some new obstacle or flight of fancy from

somebody," said Pepper. "Let's hope nobody comes up with anything too trying. I'm not in the mood."

Pushing open the door of the conference room, Hoot and Pepper joined the other members of the systems-development committee. The first item on the agenda was the response of the vice presidents to the committee's proposal on the planning and progress system. This proposal had first been requested by the planning department. The financial vice president was present to deliver this response.

"We looked at this proposal with some care," began the VP. "In outline, as you know, the system's purpose is to record the progress of orders through the plant and so provide information

THE FINANCIAL VP ADDRESSES THE MEETING

to sales, accounts, and other offices on order status. But primarily it is intended to provide the planning department with data with which they can plan order loading, routing, and so on. This would be based on accurate information on the current loads on the plants and on actual production times in various stages."

The VP looked around the table at the expectant faces. "I must confess that the scope of the system proposed made the other vice presidents somewhat nervous. They were worried by the idea of having computer terminals all over the place, and the idea of everyone having to learn to put in data on these instead of on pieces of paper. The difficulties of transition to such a system bothered them, too. On top of this, the thought of coordinating the planning of all the different plants seemed too much too soon. At first they were completely opposed to it."

"Even Reynard?" asked Hoot.

"The production VP was out of town. Unfortunately. Anyway, they thought that other projects were more pressing."

Hoot groaned. "Like putting the steel specifications book on the computer to save on printing costs, I suppose."

The VP grinned. "That was suggested."

"But if they want to save money on that, why don't they do it properly and microfilm it?"

"That's what I said," replied the VP, "but anyhow, I managed to turn talk away from such a fragmented approach to development."

"What did you do?" asked Pepper.

"I suggested that we consider ways to get started on the project without committing ourselves to the whole thing. A number of ideas were raised and we finally decided on one."

"What was that?"

"A project that could fit right onto the beginning of the original proposal—steel-melting scheduling. This would help relieve some of the work load on the planning department and make overall scheduling in the plants easier to deal with."

Despite this complete turnabout in their work, Hoot and Pepper were intrigued.

"What would that involve?" asked Pepper.

"Essentially, what the planning department does now, except

it would be done faster and more flexibly, and hopefully more cheaply. Your friend Spiky, here, from planning, will be able to give you a quick rundown on that."

"What we do," said Spiky, "is to put together orders with overlapping analyses. For example, if one customer wants an order of steel with a carbon content of between 0.15 and 0.20 percent, and another wants a carbon content of 0.17 to 0.23 percent, we could make a load of steel with a carbon content of 0.17 to 0.20 percent and satisfy both orders. That is, of course, if the silicon, manganese, phosphorus, and so on are the same in both orders. But it would be best to show you some sample orders as we do them, so why don't you come down to the planning department tomorrow morning, and I'll show you how we do it?"

"I guess we'd better," laughed Hoot. "That sounds to me as though it could get pretty complicated." He turned to the VP. "So you want us to produce a computer system that will replicate the steel-melting planning of the planning department and reduce costs, increase speed, and—what else? Increase flexibility? So that last-minute urgent orders could be quickly absorbed into the schedule?"

"Yes, that's right," replied the VP. "Why don't you get the feel of the operation and then give us a report on how you would go about it and how you would attempt to meet those objectives on costs and flexibility. Let's see how feasible it is."

"When do you want the report by?" asked Pepper.

"If you can have it ready for the next meeting, I can get it up to the VPs for their approval by the next Wednesday. Then you'll be in business."

"Let's hope that this time we stay in business," grinned Pepper.

"I'm sure you will," laughed the VP. "After all, it was their suggestion."

They covered the rest of the agenda quickly and the systems-development committee dispersed to set about its new task.

"Well, I guess we have another project," sighed Hoot, as they left the meeting.

"Yeah," replied Pepper. "I was all set to get moving on that progress system. Now we have to switch gears and think about making steel. What do you think about this change?"

"In some ways it seems OK. If you have a really complex situation, you need to break it down into manageable chunks. You need to separate out the main parts and work on them one at a time. And I guess this is a main part of the overall system."

"Yes, but we can't just look at a part in isolation. We'll have to see how it *is* connected to the overall system. In some way or other we have to dovetail this project into the rest of the operation."

"So we should look at the interconnections too," agreed Hoot. "But we have to know where to stop. Let's look just at the close connections. We don't want to follow the connections too far afield."

"No, that would be a project in itself. But somebody's got to look at the total picture sometime."

"That's what the VPs are for."

"Yeah, I guess. Well, let's get back and plan out our approach on this. We've got to figure out what questions we want to ask in this first stage."

"I suppose Spiky will do most of the talking, and the questions we ask will depend on what she says."

"Yes, I know. But we want to make sure we cover the basics, like What's the objective of this process? What are the functions and procedures involved? What principles are involved? Who does what, and when, and why? That sort of thing. Then we can get into a more specific round of questions when we know we have the essentials. See what I mean?"

"Of course I see what you mean," said Hoot a little huffily. "I do know something about the gentle art of asking questions, *and* about what questions to ask in a particular problem type."

"OK, OK," smiled Pepper. "I guess I was just getting it straight in my own head. No offense meant."

"I'm sorry. It's getting late. We should have gone home an hour ago. Look, I'll see you tomorrow morning and we'll let Spiky tell us all about steel."

"OK. 'Bye."

"Well," said Spiky the next day, "I gave you an idea yesterday of what amalgamating the orders means. But before we look at actual orders, why don't I give you a quick rundown on steel types?"

"That would be good," said Pepper, producing her large notebook.

"I'll start at the beginning and say what steel is. It's basically an iron-carbon alloy with up to 2 percent carbon in it. Then there are also other possible alloying elements such as silicon, manganese, chromium, molybdenum, nickel, tungsten, aluminum, titanium, and so on. There are two basic classes of steel— carbon steel and alloy steel. I'll talk about carbon steel first. In carbon steel, the carbon content can range from 0.10 to 10 percent, although most commonly the content is less than 1 percent. The manganese content will be between 0.30 and 1.65 percent and have a phosphorus content not exceeding 0.04 percent and a sulfur content . . ."

"Hold on, hold on," interrupted Pepper. "My pen doesn't go that fast."

Spiky laughed. "I'm just trying to tell you as much as I can today. You'll have to come back the day after tomorrow. We can't get through all this in one session. I thought I'd talk about steel specifications today, and on Thursday talk about furnace types, different kinds of products, and different heat treatments and stuff. How's that?"

"That sounds fine," said Hoot. "If there's that much to learn it's going to take a while to digest it all anyway."

"OK," said Spiky. "So, where was I?"

"Sulfur content of carbon steel."

"Oh yes—not exceeding 0.05 percent. So the AISA number C1020 would be a carbon steel with 0.18 to 0.23 percent carbon. The last digits in the number give the midpoint of the range of carbon."

"What does AISA mean?"

"Oh, American Iron and Steel Institute."

"OK." Pepper scribbled away.

"Now, carbon steel might be divided into three types. Low, medium, and high carbon.

"Low-carbon steel is what you use when you want to be able to bend it around when it's cold, like automobile bodywork or fenders. This steel has a carbon content of approximately 0.10 to 0.15 percent.

"For structural steel for bridges, or whatever, you'd want a bit more strength and you wouldn't need the steel to be so easily workable. So, a carbon content of 0.15 to 0.30 percent would be right. If you want better mechanical properties, for instance, steel for forgings and machined parts, where you'll be using heat treatments or working it cold, you'd want to go to a medium-carbon steel—0.30 to 0.60 percent.

"High-carbon steel—0.60 to 2.00 percent carbon—would be used for springs, or cutting edges on things like farm implements, where you need wear resistance. So that's the carbon steels."

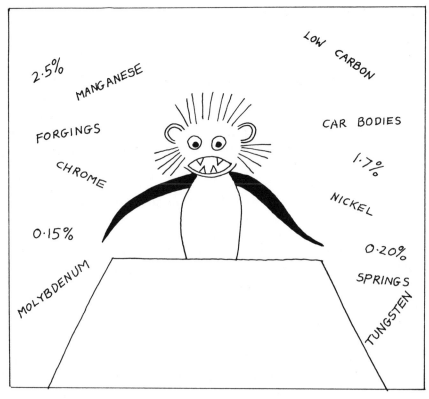

SPIKY TALKS ABOUT STEEL ANALYSIS

"That's a lot of different characteristics," said Pepper.

"Wait till you get to the alloy steels," laughed Spiky.

"Is that what you're going to talk about now?"

"Might as well. Alloy steels have a relatively high percentage of the alloying element. For example, you might have up to 18 percent or so of chromium for corrosion resistance. Alloy steels can be divided up into about six major classes. There's constructional alloy steels, high-strength low-alloy steels, stainless steels, tool steels, heat-resistant steels, and silicon steels. Most of these alloys have a carbon content of considerably less than 1 percent. Let's look at them one at a time. What did I say first?"

"Constructional."

"Oh, yes. If you want strength and ductility and want the steel to respond to heat treatment, you might want to use constructional steel. The alloying elements in this would usually fall into the range of 1 to 4 percent. Things like tungsten, or titanium, cobalt, niobium, aluminum, zirconium, are added for different reasons. Now, the high-strength low-alloy steels are stronger than the constructional, relatively low in cost, but are not meant for heat treatment. What's next?"

"Stainless."

"Corrosion resistance is the chief thing here. Nearly all stainless steels contain at least 11.5 percent chromium. Some have large amounts of manganese or nickel, too, which improves their working properties and also adds to corrosion resistance. For example, in the chromium-nickel steels one of the most widely used is type 302, or '18-8' stainless. This has, let me see now, yes, 0.15 percent carbon, 18 percent chromium, 8 percent nickel. On the other hand, type 202 has 0.15 percent carbon, 7.5 to 10 percent manganese, 4 to 6 percent nickel, and 17 to 19 percent chromium. You'll be able to see those kinds of specs when we look at the order sheets."

"The customer orders the steel down to that level of specification?"

"Oh, no, not usually. They may specify a copper or tin range or something, but usually they order by the steel type number and the sales office prepares the order sheet for the planning department from the steel specification book."

"Oh, yes, we've heard about that," said Hoot.

Spiky grinned and went on. "Heat-resistant steels are the kind they use for jet engines and rocket motors. They're more highly alloyed than the stainless steels."

"You missed tool steels," said Pepper, skimming through her notes.

"Tool steels. Well, you know what they are for. Cutting, forging, extruding, sawing, and other heavy-duty processes. Here again, I guess, there are two or three types. There are carbon-tool steels, with 0.60 to 1.40 percent carbon. There are alloy-tool steels, with chromium, molybdenum, tungsten, or vanadium added to increase wear resistance and help the steel keep a good cutting edge. And there are high-speed steels. These are designed for hardness and abrasion resistance at high temperatures, like what you get when you're cutting stainless steel, for example. Anyway something like '18-4-1' can hold its cutting edge for quite a long time, even at temperatures as hot as 1000°F."

"What's '18-4-1'?"

"Ah. That has 18 percent tungsten, 4 percent chromium and 1 percent vanadium. Sometimes high-speed steels have cobalt added to help out with hardness and abrasion. OK, Pepper, what did I miss?"

"The last one was silicon steel."

"Right. Sometimes called electrical steel because it's what is used in things like transformers, electric motors, and generators. These steels contain 0.5 to 5.0 percent silicon for high electrical resistance. For example, there's Hadfield silicon steel, which has about 3 percent silicon and less than 0.1 percent carbon. So how's that for a start?"

Pepper raised her eyebrows. "It's a lot to remember."

"Oh, it'll all fall into place," said Spiky. "Things start to stick in your mind. You'll soon be looking at an order and knowing what kind of steel it is. In fact, let's look at these orders. It'll give you an idea of what the specifications actually look like. Here."

Hoot and Pepper looked over the order sheet that Spiky indicated.

"What's all this down here?" asked Hoot.

"Oh, that's the heat treatment and stuff. I'll tell you about that on Thursday."

They examined a few order forms. Spiky promised to have copies of the orders for the last couple of months made so they could get the feel of steel making.

"You'd better have a comprehensive tour of the rolling mills tomorrow. I'll ask the Hawk to tell you about it all and show you through. There are a lot of different ways to produce steel, and that affects the scheduling, so you should familiarize yourself with that. If you can do that tomorrow, I'll set it up with the Hawk."

Accordingly, the rolling-mills tour was set up for the next morning. On the day after that, Thursday, Hoot and Pepper were to return for more information on scheduling of steel melting.

"Hi, you guys," called the Hawk as Pepper and Hoot came through the door of the rolling-mills office. "Come in and sit down. Spiky says you want to know all about blooms and billets."

"Blooms and what?" asked Hoot.

The Hawk laughed. "More technicalities, eh? I'll bet Spiky gave you a good rundown on making steel. She really knows her stuff. Never known a woman so excited about steel."

"She told us all about different types of steel yesterday," said Pepper. "Tomorrow she's going to tell us about the different kinds of furnaces."

"Crash course, eh?" said the Hawk. "Well, my story begins when we get the ingots from the molds. They sit in what we call soaking pits, where the temperature is held at between 1150 and 1315°C. You've probably seen the lids roll back and that great set of tongs on the overhead crane pick out an ingot and set it down on the rollers of the primary mill."

"Yes, we were watching an ingot being rolled the other day," said Hoot. "We often watch as we go through the mill. I didn't realize they were so hot, though. No wonder it's so warm on the catwalk."

"Right. So you've probably noticed those ingots being rolled to different sizes. There are three basic shapes. These are blooms, billets, and slabs. Blooms are square or oblong, with a cross section of six inches by six inches to twelve inches by twelve inches. Billets are smaller in section than a bloom. They're between two inches by two inches and five inches by five inches. A slab is an oblong. It's between two inches and six inches thick and between two feet and six feet wide. Come along and I'll show you."

They all went into the rolling mills and up onto the catwalk. As they did so, a long, thick piece of steel was snaking away from the primary mill.

"What would you say that was?" asked the Hawk.

"Is it a bloom?" offered Hoot.

"That's right. It's going to the finishing mills now to be made into a rail."

"For a railroad?"

"That's right. Let's watch what they do to it."

They walked along the catwalk to the finishing mill, which handled rail sections. The Hawk pointed to a couple of men with large tongs standing by the rollers.

"Have you seen what they do?" asked the Hawk.

"Yes," replied Pepper. "When the steel comes through out of one of the grooves in the roller, the men with the tongs guide the bar back into the next groove and the roller reverses and squeezes it down a bit further."

"That's right. The steel is reduced in section gradually and finally takes up the shape of a rail."

"It gets a lot longer as they do it," remarked Hoot.

"Yeah, that's why they have those long run-out roller beds. See that?"

Hoot and Pepper turned their heads to follow the pointing finger. They saw a blackened hole in the brick wall at the end of the run-out bed.

"What happened?"

"Miscalculation," said the Hawk. "Calculations for the length of the run-out were made before we started the twenty-ton ingots from the electric arc furnaces. Naturally the output from the bigger ingots squeezed out to longer rails. So, the first time we rolled them, the red-hot rail hit the wall and went straight on through. We've just left the hole there. It works."

"I'd never have thought of that," said Hoot.

"Yeah, there are a lot of things to keep in mind when you start changing things around. You guys had better know your stuff if you're going to be working on melting scheduling. You're lucky you've got Spiky backing you up."

"You're right," said Pepper. "The complexity of the job makes me nervous enough. But the thought of making mistakes involving twenty tons of white-hot steel flailing around horrifies me."

"Don't worry," laughed the Hawk. "We won't let anyone screw up this operation too badly. What else can I tell you?"

A ROLLING MILLS OVERSIGHT

"Why do you make different sizes of steel sections in the primary mills? These blooms and billets."

"Ah, yes. Well, it depends on what finished sizes you want. The bigger finished products would be made from blooms. Smaller-section things like bars, as you've seen, get made from billets."

"What about slabs?"

"Oh, they're for things like plate and sheet."

"So let's just go over that again, can we?" asked Pepper. "Let's take the blooms first. What finishing mills do they go to?"

"OK. Blooms can be made into tube rounds—that's for seamless pipe. They go for big structural shapes too, like girders and I beams."

"And rails."

"Right."

"What about slabs?" Pepper asked next.

"Well, they could go to the plate mill to be made into plate, which could then be made into large-diameter pipes. Or they could be made into hot- or cold-rolled sheet in the sheet mill. Then, there's skelp."

"Skelp?" laughed Hoot. "I thought that grew in the sea."

"That's kelp, idiot," grinned Pepper.

The Hawk laughed. "That goes to make welded pipe or tubing."

"So that leaves billets."

"Billets go to make bars, rods, and tube rounds."

"Tube rounds?" asked Hoot. "Didn't you say they were made from blooms?"

"Yes they are. Blooms are for bigger tubes."

"Oh."

"What else can I tell you? I have to get back to the office now, so I can't show you round the finishing mills. But if you've more questions to ask, we can do that in the office."

"Perhaps you could point out the main finishing mills and we'll walk around for a while to get the feel of things. Then can we come and ask questions if we have any?"

"OK, fine." The Hawk told them how to see sheet being rolled, bars being cold-drawn, and girders being rolled.

"See you later."

Hoot and Pepper set off around the finishing mills and watched the different products being made. As they strolled into the plate mill they bumped into the foreman. They introduced themselves and told the foreman what they were about. He showed them over the mill and its workings.

"We're not making as much plate as we used to, now that we're not getting any more internal orders," remarked the foreman at one point.

"Internal orders?" asked Pepper. "What are they?"

"Oh, they're like customer orders, but where the customer is ourselves. We make plate for our own stock, or rather we used to, and shipped it to the plate stores in the different locations."

Hoot and Pepper looked at each other. They hadn't heard about internal orders. They both were wondering when these orders originated and how they fitted into the flow of other orders.

Then Pepper asked, "Why aren't you getting any more plate orders?"

"Because they've decided to centralize all the plate stores. Just keep one and close down all the others to save space and manpower. Since they weren't keeping much plate in each store, they thought it would be cheaper to ship the plate from a central location when it's needed."

"Yeah, I can see that," agreed Hoot.

They completed their tour of the plate mill and walked back to their office.

"We must talk to Spiky tomorrow about these internal orders," said Hoot. "I hope this doesn't mean a separate procedure has to be taken into account."

"If the situation is like what the foreman described, and it's a regular order where we are the customer, it shouldn't affect what we're working on. But Spiky'll know all that."

They busied themselves recording what they'd learned that day and prepared for the next day's investigations, making a note of issues, ideas, and problems they needed to discuss.

When they met with Spiky, the first thing they asked about was the internal order system. Spiky gave them a quick rundown on how the various different types of orders originated, how they came into the planning department, and where they went after that.

"But what's this about the plate stores?" Spiky asked.

Hoot and Pepper related the plate-mill foreman's story. Spiky was perturbed. "I'll follow that up," she said. "There's something not quite right about that." She made a note and turned back to her friends.

"Well, let's carry on with the saga of steel," she grinned. "Furnaces. We have three types scattered around the various plants. Right here, as you know, we have the electric-arc furnaces. But at East Vale we have acid open-hearth and at Fir Town we have basic open-hearth."

"What are they?"

"Well, basic open-hearth is a kind of huge bath with a lid on it. Furnace sizes range from 40 tons to 600 tons per heat, but they average around 200 tons. We have a couple of 200-tonners, and two 50s. These furnaces can use ore that has too high a phosphorus content to be made in the acid open-hearth. The basic open-hearth process makes it possible to use pig iron with any phosphorus content up to 1 percent, and to do it pretty economically."

"What's acid open-hearth?" asked Hoot.

"Oh, it's like basic, but it's an older system and has been pretty much superseded. Basic is better able to remove phosphorus and sulfur impurities."

"And the electric-arc furnaces are those huge pots with the three big electrodes sticking in through the lid?"

"That's right. The electric-arc furnaces are charged almost entirely with scrap metal, as opposed to iron ore, and they melt by electrical resistance. We have two 100-tonners. Electric-arc furnaces produce nearly all the high-quality steels—the stainless, tool, and special alloy steels that are needed by the aircraft, transportation, food-processing, and chemical industries. But this process is more expensive, so we try not to use it for more common grades of steel. Then again, sometimes it pays to make some orders by a more expensive process to avoid other expense complications in later processes that the steel goes through. We want to avoid trucking an order all over the place. The various types of furnaces, many of them in other places, the different products, like the ones you saw yesterday, the different heat treatments and cooling rates, all have to be considered when you plan where the steel order will be melted and where it will go next."

At this point Hoot and Pepper had a number of questions concerning furnace capacities and running costs, the factors involved in what orders can go with what, and ways to get the order through as fast as possible while minimizing costs and maximizing plant utilization. They tried to ask questions that would ensure that they gained a clear idea of most of the interactions, interconnections, and ramifications of the steel-melting and -scheduling processes. After two long hours they felt they'd had enough, and they left Spiky to the complexities of scheduling.

When Hoot and Pepper returned to their office, they had a great deal of information to digest.

"We've got to organize all this information so we can get the central processes clear in our minds," said Hoot.

"Probably the best way to get an overall picture of this is to make a flowchart," said Pepper. "If we do that we can clearly indicate each decision point in each process. A flowchart will help us to organize all this material and to pick up on any parts we've missed, like decision points with none or only one of the choices shown, and things like that."

"But there's too much detail to put down on a skeleton arrangement like a flowchart. We need some way of documenting all that stuff about furnace types and different steel specifications."

"Sure. But we could put a note on the flowchart at the appropriate point to refer us to a descriptive passage attached to the flowchart. Anyway, if we're going to do a detailed flowchart, a lot of that information will appear at choice points. For example, 'If steel is type X and melted at furnace type Y, then process Z not required,' or something like that."

"Hmmm," responded Hoot, "perhaps you're right. I just wouldn't want to be using a technique that is too cumbersome or time-consuming for what we're trying to do here."

"I know. But since this is going to be written as a computer program, this degree of detail and precision seems to fit."

"Yeah," grinned Hoot. "I guess I was just trying to avoid the concentrated effort that will be required to organize all this information at the same level of detail. I know already that there are some pretty fuzzy areas in the information we have. There were some points where I just didn't make the connections at all."

"Well, this flowchart will force us to ask questions at the fuzzy points. We can't have arrows that point nowhere."

After a couple of hours they had the skeleton of a flowchart roughed out. As they had expected, there were a number of arrows that pointed nowhere, a number of choice points where it wasn't clear what was being decided about, and a few mysterious gaps.

HOOT AND PEPPER GATHER PLENTY OF INFORMATION

"Looks like we'll have to see Spiky a few more times, Pepper."

"Yeah, And it's also beginning to look as though this is pretty closely interwoven with our old planning and progress system. If we are to decide what orders to load onto what furnaces, we have to know what's already being processed there and further down the line. Otherwise we could have bottlenecks."

"To schedule this stuff properly we must know what orders are already in process and where they are; how long the various processes take; what delays, changes, shutdowns, or extra capacity there might be."

They sat and thought about that for a while.

"Look, this doesn't make sense," said Hoot, exasperated. "We can't detail the whole corporation's operations from start to finish before we produce this first project. There's got to be a way to see the overall process and yet pull out a small part of it."

"True. How does the planning department schedule things now without the planning and progress system?" said Pepper. She grinned as Hoot saw his mistake. "There *is* a way of knowing where things are. It may not be all automated and tidy, but the planning department does have feedback from the mills and melting shops."

Hoot groaned. "You're right. I've been looking at all this from one angle for too long. I'm failing to see the obvious. I need a change of pace."

"It's almost time to go home, anyway. But you're right about one thing. It would be a good idea to have an overall systems-development plan for the big picture. Since things are so closely interwoven, any decisions about how we produce this computing system will affect things further down the line when, or if, they decide to set up a planning and progress system. We can't do it all now, obviously. At the same time, we can't ignore the interconnected issues. We really should have some overall plan, at least in outline."

"Hmmm. Well, that's two issues. One, how should systems development be done at this corporation? Two, how should we do this particular project? As far as I'm concerned, both of those will have to wait until tomorrow. My mind is buzzing with all this new stuff. I need time to let it all sink in."

So saying, they agreed to call it a day and resume wrestling with the problem in the morning.

The next day Hoot came bursting into the office, full of enthusiasm. "Well," he said before Pepper even had time to say hi, "it sure helps to let a problem settle for a while. Listen. This is the way I see it."

Pepper looked at Hoot and concealed a yawn. She hadn't had her morning coffee yet and wasn't under the great stimulus to action that you get from the feeling of having made a breakthrough in a thorny problem. But she listened attentively as Hoot went on. "We need to look at how the problem is defined. We have been getting bogged down because our view of the scope of the immediate project is shifting. We need to pin down more clearly what our immediate problem is, and then, how the problem relates to everything else. We need to deal with those two issues separately."

Pepper began to wake up. "I see what you mean. You're saying that in a sense we are dealing with this scheduling problem as a sub-problem of the bigger overall problem of order production. What we now have to do is to divide this sub-problem into two parts, too. The first part is the sub-problem itself: scheduling of steel melting in the technical sense. The second part is the interactions of the sub-problem with the remainder of the problem: how to put the orders together in a way that is both technically correct and takes into account plant loadings and progress and so on."

"Right. Maybe we can divide what we're doing into two parts like that. We could produce a computer system that can handle all the technical details involved in putting together orders, and the planning department could somehow provide the computer system with the constraints of loading and progress in the way they do now."

"Hmm." Pepper thought about that for a while. "There's another way of looking at this. We could put together a pilot project first. I mean, let's produce the programs for steel melting. We'll use these same orders the planning department used over the last two months. Then we'll see how the computer version compares with the actual job that Spiky and her friends did. This would increase our knowledge of the process, and help us figure out and test the basic principles whereby the process fits into the larger picture.''

"Oh. I see. Then we'd be able to put together a better set of programs enabling the planning department to work *with* our system and guide it in the light of their knowledge of plant loads and so forth.''

"Yes,'' said Pepper. "Then we could gradually work toward a planning and progress system in easy stages.''

They sat and talked through the concept some more. "We should go and talk to Spiky about this now and make sure we've gotten it all straight and that our idea makes sense,'' suggested Pepper. Hoot agreed. When they phoned, Spiky was able to make time to see them right away, so they scurried over to the planning department.

"Hi, you guys,'' said Spiky, as Hoot and Pepper arrived. "How's the master plan going?''

"We need your advice on this idea of ours,'' said Hoot, and proceeded to explain their two-stage scheme.

"That sounds OK in theory,'' said Spiky. "The only thing is we have to make sure that the planning input on plant loads and so on isn't too cumbersome. This system is supposed to help us, not hinder us. Had you intended the computer system to make an initial trial scheduling for us to adjust with our knowledge, or did you think we'd supply the computer system with some initial constraints, or what?''

"That's part of what we want to discuss with you,'' said Pepper. They talked about the various ways in which the planning department and the computer system could work together to produce the best scheduling as fast and conveniently as possible and at the same time reduce the work load of the planning department. Eventually they worked out a way for the experimental pilot system to operate, and a way that it might fit in the plans for future expansion into a planning and progress system. They agreed that an overall outline plan for later expansion should form a background against which the pilot scheme would take place. They also agreed that, to keep the whole scheme on track, their proposal for the systems development committee should request approval for both the pilot system and the overall outline plan.

"Oh, and guess what!'' Spiky said after they had agreed on

an outline for the proposal for the committee.

"What?"

"I went and checked out what was happening with those plate-mill internal orders. What has happened is really embarrassing for the stores controller. I mentioned the problem to Reynard, the production VP, and he looked into what was going on. When he found out he was furious. I guess it would have been better if I'd talked to Jake, the stores controller, first. But you know how difficult to deal with he is."

"But what happened?" insisted Hoot.

"You won't believe it," Spiky replied. "I wouldn't have myself, but it really did happen."

"What did, what did?!" shrieked Pepper and Hoot in exasperation.

REYNARD IS FURIOUS

"Well you know how they decided to close down all the plate stores except one? OK. The stores controller left it up to the individual store managers to decide, on the basis of location, space, and manpower, which one to keep open. The unbelievable thing is that somehow, somewhere along the line, the decision didn't get clarified and *all* the plate stores were closed down. Now we're running out of plate and, if the issue isn't resolved soon, we'll be shutting down jobs because we can't supply ourselves with plate."

"No wonder Jake is embarrassed. That really looks bad."

"Let's hope he's in a better mood when our proposal comes up at their meeting," said Pepper.

"Yeah," agreed Spiky. "He's pretty sure to make trouble for us, even if he doesn't know it was I who mentioned it to Reynard."

"That's right," said Hoot. "You remember the inventory control project?"

"I'll never forget it," laughed Spiky, "You'd think the systems-development committee was planning a revolution rather than making stock ordering a lot easier and safer."

"Well, he got the proposal thrown out," said Hoot. "Maybe he'll do the same to ours out of sheer exasperation."

"We must make sure that there are no loose ends in this proposal then," reflected Pepper. "We can't afford to give him an excuse to attack it."

Thus chastened, they returned to their office to put together the most foolproof proposal they could.

Hoot and Pepper's report, with the endorsement of Spiky, received the financial VP's blessing at the next systems-development committee meeting.

"We're pretty certain to get opposition from Jake, both at the VPs' meeting, and behind the scenes," said the financial VP when Spiky had told her story of how the plate-stores fiasco had been unveiled. "What we can't predict is the means he'll use to attack—only that it will be skillful and tricky. He won't use just one approach. He'll back it up with something on a different tack. He'll try to push us off balance and make us flustered so that we contribute to our destruction. He'll also be working behind the scenes, persuading individual members, with arguments directed toward their special interests, to oppose us. As far as I can see, the report as it stands is pretty strong. You don't ask for too much. It can be done in stages and the project could be stopped at some places without ruining its contribution up to that point. I'm not quite sure how he'll mount his attack. I'm going to have to look into that. In the meantime, you guys had better be on top of this thing. Don't leave any loopholes. I can see it now: 'How can we entrust a system as critical as this to people who didn't even spot such and such?' Make sure you know all this inside out and upside down."

The meeting broke up, with Hoot and Pepper leaving more nervous than when they came in.

"Phew," breathed Hoot. "It isn't enough just to think up some neat ideas and make a good case for them."

"No, it isn't," replied Pepper. "A problem isn't solved when you think up a solution. You can say it's solved only when it doesn't exist anymore. So I guess we have a long haul yet before we can breathe easy. We'd better prepare for the lion's den."

"Just for once I'd like to see how it feels to be a lion," muttered Hoot.

In the couple of days before the meeting, little pieces of information began to trickle back about the stores controller's private influencing sessions with various people. Apparently he was contending that the report indicated that things were going to be much more complicated than before. He was trying to persude people that the planning department's scheduling work was vital to the corporation's survival, that, in order to work properly, this proposed melting scheduling system would have to be fed by the progress system that everyone had previously rejected as too complicated. He was also asserting that the planning department was doing a fine job and that there was no need to upset the corporation with experimental systems and to gamble with the corporation's survival.

Eagerly, Hoot and Pepper gathered the different angles the stores controller had taken, prepared a detailed response to each one, and rehearsed each other in various versions of these responses.

"We had better keep in touch with the financial VP so we

know about other possible attacks," warned Pepper.

"I know. Even though it looks as though we have all his points taken care of, the uncertainty is giving me the jitters. I'll be glad when it's all over."

"Well, it will be in two days. Till then we'll just have to take some comfort in the fact that we're really learning the system inside out."

The day of the meeting finally arrived. Just as the VP had predicted, Jake was all set to push them off balance. Instead of attacking the report that Hoot and Pepper had prepared, he started with an assault on computing techniques and launched into a tirade against planning. Hoot and Pepper's careful preparation didn't help them.

"We must beware of being dominated and bewitched by so-

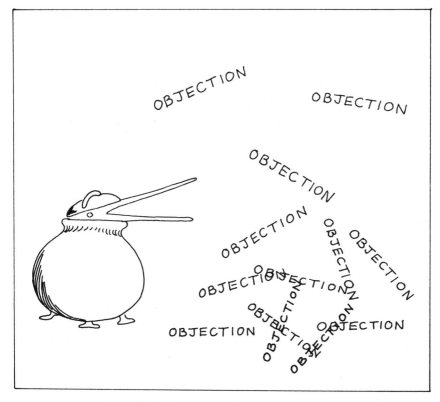

JAKE SAYS HIS PIECE

phisticated techniques," insisted Jake. "It's one thing for data processing to serve us by doing our accounting and payroll. It's another thing for the mystique of computers to blindfold us. Clever techniques are impressive, but excessive reliance on technique can stifle the corporation's dynamism."

Attempts to interrupt the tirade and set the stores controller's remarks in a different perspective were drowned out as Jake warmed to his theme. His energetic attack was fuelled by the embarrassment of the plate-stores fiasco. Furthermore, he knew that some others present had misgivings about the computer invasion. His rhetoric served to blunt the distinction between the computer as a bad thing and the *misuse* of the computer as a bad thing. Some of his points were good ones.

"People become overconfident," he went on. "People see a computer forecast as somehow magical. They accept it and don't think about the possibility of error in these forecasts. And speaking of erroneous forecasts, that's part of the trouble with this trend toward more formal planning. You pick a particular view of the future and organize around this. "This approach is inflexible. A company doesn't grow if it's inflexible."

Protests that brought up the issue of contingency planning and alternate targets were submerged as Jake hurried off on another tangent.

"You spend so much of your time planning for what *might* happen that you overlook what *is* happening. Nothing gets done in the present because everyone's thinking about the future. And what's more, too much effort and manpower go into keeping all the documentation and progress charts up to date. Or, you spend all your time searching for more and more information in a false quest for certainty before you dare to act. And what do you do about things you hadn't planned for?"

He stared around the room triumphantly. "No. Give me the on-the-spot man who can act decisively in a tight situation."

Jake sat down. For a while nobody spoke. Where could they start? The stores controller had brought up so many issues, glossed over so many fine points, and introduced so many half-truths and diversions that it would take a project team to produce a rebuttal.

Finally, the chairman sighed and said, "Unfortunately, our

specialist in planning, the vice president for production, couldn't be here today. I'm sure he could say a great deal about the stores controller's remarks. I think the stores controller has raised some interesting points that should be discussed at our next meeting. In the meantime, however, we must respond more directly to the systems-development committee's proposal."

Another wrangle ensued, with Jake insisting that it all be delayed until the planning questions were resolved, and others insisting that a pilot scheme couldn't do any harm and that the systems people should be allowed to produce one. Jake said that if time and money were to be spent, it should be on something that would help regardless of what happened. Other proposals, covering a limited-progress data-recording system that could serve a number of different purposes, were suggested. The chairman finally adjourned the meeting and placed the complex issue on the agenda of the next meeting. As far as Hoot and Pepper were concerned, nothing had been settled. They left the meeting and went back to their office.

"This isn't a very satisfactory state of affairs," grumbled Hoot. "How can we do anything productive or even rewarding against a background that lacks pattern and coherence? All this uncertainty and changing of direction is quite distressing. I'm beginning to feel that I'd work on any system, no matter how silly, if it would keep still and allow us to work our way through to the end of it."

"I agree," said Pepper. "Let's talk to the financial VP and see if we can get some firmer guidelines. If the whole issue of planning is going to be discussed, the place of systems development and data processing should be clarified, too."

"This is a long way from steel specifications," sighed Hoot. "How come we always get embroiled in deeper and deeper problems? It all seems so simple when you start a project."

Pepper laughed. "You're right," she said. "But that's a mistake a lot of people make. They don't realize that part of solving a problem, which is what a project really is, is to *clarify* all these interconnected issues and establish where the project sits in relation to them all. Only then, when you have a precise definition of the problem, can you proceed to develop solutions. If you produce an answer that doesn't reflect the effect of the interconnected issues on the project, the answer is going to fail as soon as it's plugged into the actual situation."

"I guess you're right. It's just that I want to get on with something concrete. I suppose Jake would accuse me of wanting just to deal with certainties."

"Well, that's not quite what he said. But, I know what you mean."

"I'm not so sure I know what Jake meant half of the time."

"No. Nor am I. Look. Let's call the financial VP and ask him to meet with us about our situation."

"OK," Hoot replied wearily. "Another round of negotiations."

The meeting was set for the next morning. Pepper began to think through some of the issues. Hoot had a cup of coffee.

Hoot set the meeting off to a quick start by saying that he and Pepper were perturbed by the way their work was turning out.

"We need a clearer picture of where we are going," he said. "What do the vice presidents think of our operation? Is there a strategy that underlies systems development here? Or is it up to the various departments and divisions to make proposals to the systems-development committee? Who decides what data-processing projects should be proposed? What criteria are there for assessing these proposals, other than the analysis that the systems-development committee does?"

The financial vice president looked thoughtful. Then he said, "I guess we really haven't given any thought to strategic direction for a long time. When we first set this up, before you and Pepper came to work here, we planned to computerize some of the basic tedious routines in which speed and accuracy and ease of manipulation were the prime requirements. Payroll, general ledger, general accounting, basic functions like that."

"But the inventory-control system was shot down," remarked Pepper.

"I know. I think that might have been the point at which our neglect of development directions first became apparent, but we haven't really recognized that yet."

He paused. "I was thinking a little about that last night and thought it might be a good idea to get Reynard down here."

"The production vice president?"

"Yes. I figured things might take a strategic turn. And as a planning and strategy advocate, Reynard's help would be invaluable here. I'll tell him we're ready. He said he'd be available around ten o'clock."

Not long after that, the production vice president had joined them and was listening to Hoot and Pepper's view of the situation. Now Pepper had picked up on the theme and was suggesting a principle to incorporate into their thinking about the role of systems development.

"We should look at information as a *resource*," she said. "The corporation's information is a resource like any other resource—plant, capital, inventory, or whatever. What you get out of it depends on how you use it. If you don't take care of it, it will begin to malfunction. Information isn't just about what *has* happened, but about what *is* happening and, equally or more important, about what *will* happen or *might* happen. If information is cared for and employed properly, it can keep the corporation flexible and responsive, rather than sluggish, half-blind, and always acting after the fact."

The production VP laughed. He was thinking of the plate stores. Pepper went on, "Good information is vital to planning and flexible response. Good information-systems development and planned action go hand in hand."

"Maybe you should say competent planned action," smiled Reynard. "But carry on."

"If we plan systems development around the concept of information-as-a-resource, and look to the creation of a comprehensive and flexible corporate data-base or information pool, we can avoid this kind of piecemeal operation. Now we work in fragments and end up going around and around in circles. Our projects may be more expensive than they need be. They may be duplicating each other, or overlapping, or stopping and starting and changing around. There are no clear guidelines, so there is no way to know whether one direction is any better than another. Hence, indecision, changes, and confusion. It's beginning to seem to Hoot and me that the main problem here isn't deciding which project to pick, but deciding what the basic objectives of the systems development of the corporation are."

"That's right," said Hoot. "We must operate in some kind of a framework rather than in a void."

"I can agree with that," said Reynard.

"Before you came, Reynard, I was saying that we've lost touch with systems development strategy since the earlier days," said the financial VP.

Reynard smiled. "Worse than that, really. *Policy* is the problem. Our overall planning has been becoming a little fuzzy of late. It's no longer being done at a policy level, more at a tactical level." He looked at Hoot and Pepper. "Hmm. Maybe I should explain."

He settled back in his chair. The financial VP stared at the

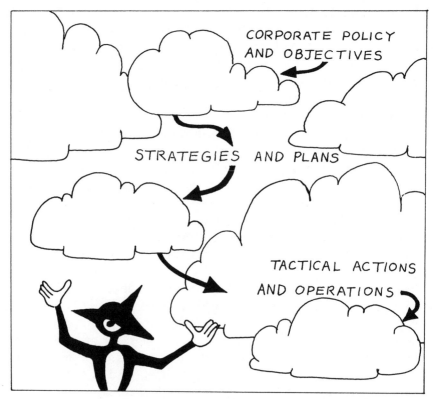

A CLOUDY ISSUE FOR REYNARD

ceiling. He'd heard it all before. The production VP began his explanation. "You can look at planning on three levels—policy, strategy, and tactics. At the policy level you're looking at basic goals, based on anticipated and examined future probabilities, so that priorities can be set for the investment of both financial and human resources. At the strategic level you're looking at alternate options for achieving the specific goals you've set— how to get the business to achieve its investment priorities. Then, at the tactical level, you're looking at the operations themselves—how to implement a selected strategy option with coherent and integrated programs. I agree, Pepper and Hoot, that your operation doesn't have any strategic direction."

"I'm glad you see it that way," Pepper said. "Without an overall strategic direction, regular decision making and problem solving is more difficult because you have to start from scratch every time, figuring out where you want to go and how."

"That's true," said the financial VP. "Under a strategic umbrella, many directions or ground rules are preselected, and vacillating can be avoided. Problems can be defined faster, their scope assessed faster, and decisions made more quickly."

"Right," said Reynard. "Once systems development begins to rise above the level of operational stuff, as you're suggesting it should with your information-as-a-resource concept and with your idea of blending it into planning, systems development becomes confused because it has no context in which to operate. If we were planning and thinking at a higher level, we'd be able to integrate forecasting, goals, policy, information, planning, change, and action into an orchestrated effort by the corporation at all levels—policy, management, and operations. And this integration could be backed up at all levels of strategic and tactical planning, and decision making, by information systems and analytic and projective tools."

"Hmm," said Hoot. "This is beginning to get a little too abstract for me."

"Maybe I can make it clearer for you. For some time now I've been working on a proposal for a different corporate structure. The present systems-development situation plus the plate-stores fiasco might just give me the leverage I need to get the proposal into operation."

"I thought you were up to something, Reynard," grinned the financial VP. "Let's hear your latest scheme."

"OK. It's like this. I want to introduce what I call the focal-problem team approach as the right hand of the policy makers. This innovation would involve setting up a new division, though not necessarily hiring any different people. This division would be charged with examining all the future implications and ramifications of our proposed policy and strategy alternatives, maybe using extrapolation, scenarios, simulations, and so on. Their purpose would be to forecast problems. This identification of potential or inevitable future problems would give the corporation more time to adjust in order to make the most flexible and advantageous response."

"A kind of reconnaissance patrol into the future?" suggested the financial VP.

"Exactly. Then we'd be ready to go for broke no matter which way the future unfolded. Another thing I'd want this division to do would be to look at the *interactions* between problem areas. Too often, we neglect to look at how different problems affect each other. We treat each one in isolation. Our problems are generally interlinked to some extent. We must recognize this.

"So, we could work into the future to increase both our choices and our control over events. My organization chart would have the board of directors, the chief executive officer, and us lowly VPs operating at the policy level. Then the chart would branch. On one leg there'd be the corporate development division—my focal-problem team—who'd be looking for problems and also developing strategic planning for these."

"Wouldn't the VPs be responsible for strategic planning?" asked the financial VP.

"I was hoping that at least some of the VPs would be involved in the focal-problem team. And of course all strategic planning would need the involvement of all the VPs in some capacity. OK? Then, on the other branch of the chart, there'd be the same operating divisions as there are now. They would be guided by policy and strategic planning, but would work out their own tactics. Ideally, these divisions would also provide input to the focal-problem team. Against that kind of background it should be possible for Pepper and Hoot to gain a better idea of where systems development should be going, and consequently what kind of a corporate data base is needed, what kinds of management support tools, and so on."

"Won't the stores controller campaign against this idea, as he has against all the other planning systems?" queried Hoot.

"What do you say to that, Reynard?" asked the financial VP. "It's not good enough just to have a fine idea and a sound solution. If you are unable to implement your solution, you might as well not have it. You're going to have to treat the implementation of this solution as a problem in its own right, and part of that problem is how to deal with the stores controller."

"I know. But Jake has decided to mount his attack on the basis of the idea that planning must be cumbersome and inflexible. The strength of my proposal is exactly that this focal-problem approach to planning will lead to greater flexibility and adaptability than would otherwise be possible. Planning has many obvious advantages. Its dangers can be circumvented once you've acknowledged that there *are* dangers. Planning isn't only looking at the implications for the future that the present events hold, in order to avoid the short-sighted mistakes we so often make. It's also looking at the present implications of future events. If you can see that a particular event is going to take place, you should look at the present circumstances that will give rise to the event. You may wish to modify these circumstances and thus modify the future situation. We need to create policy and have it as our guide, but we need to create it and review it in the light of both present and future events and their ramifications."

"But," said the financial VP, "since we will always be dealing with uncertainties, contingency planning and skillful and flexible action and thinking at all levels are vital, too."

"Yes, that's right. That's another resource," the production VP said to Hoot and Pepper, "our problem-solving skills and their development."

"So you're going to say," said the financial VP, "that in the context you're outlining, planning is definitely going to enhance flexibility rather than detract from it?"

"Absolutely."

"Well, that should give Hoot and Pepper and the systems-development committee some comfort."

They talked more about the implications of Reynard's approach for systems development and the two VPs promised to do their best to get some guidelines laid down soon. Hoot and Pepper left the meeting feeling fairly optimistic.

"Well, whichever way this goes," Pepper said, "it looks as though the systems-development effort will be provided with some direction and some objectives. Given a policy background against which we can act, systems work can be more easily understood and linked to the corporation's growth directions."

Hoot said, "You remember what we were saying earlier about getting the definition of the problem straight? That's what we're all still doing here. We're struggling to define the problem. It's

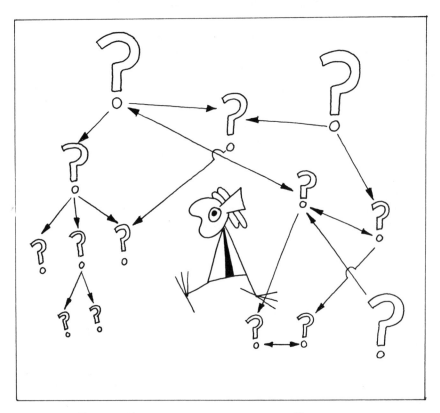

BUT WHAT IS THE PROBLEM?

a complex problem with many fuzzy aspects. I hope that the committee treats it as such. If they take the wrong approach to the problem, they'll end up with an even more confusing situation than we already have."

"That's true. You know, to some degree all problems contain other smaller ones, or are contained, like nested boxes, in other bigger ones. This apparent hierarchy of difficulties isn't all bad. It offers the possibility of solving a smaller problem by solving a larger problem because you are changing the context in which the smaller problem is set. Here we might have solved the problem of erratic and fragmented systems development by changing the corporate planning and strategy background against which the systems effort takes place. Giving form to the larger problem in turn gave form to the smaller problem contained within it. This is why it is always important to look around the problem as well as at it before deciding which is the best level at which to attack it."

"Yes," said Hoot, "but what *is* the problem? Is it dealing with the complexities of scheduling steel melting? Is it deciding whether to work on melting scheduling, or the order progress system, or a planning *and* progress system? Or, is it setting up systems-development priorities and implementing them? Or, is it incorporating at the proper level the concept of information-as-a-resource? Or, is it determining formal corporate-planning structure and directions? Or, is it fitting progress and planning systems into the context of corporate strategy and enmeshing systems development in that structure? Which problems are our problems, and which belong to someone else? Are all these issues problems at different levels? How are these issues interrelated? Could the problem be something else?"

What do *you* think?

MICRO-STRATEGIES

Micro-Strategy 1. Taking a first look
In taking a first look at a problem, you can gain an overview of the situation by reviewing the information you have, and by considering where and how to find additional information.

1. What do you already know about this situation? What can you quickly find out?
2. Where else could you find information about the situation?
3. What sources that you've never thought of before or that you have previously considered and rejected might be available?
4. What outlandish possibilities are there? Could these be turned to good account?
5. What might happen next? In the near future? In the long term?
6. What are the different shapes the future might take? What actions might trigger these future events? What information would indicate the direction being taken?
7. Are you looking far enough ahead?
8. What do you have to do to unearth, detect, or develop information about:
—areas of accelerating growth?
—evolutionary, developmental, or historical patterns for the overall situation and/or separate parts?
—interactions between parts, people, factors, or attitudes?
—things that are part of the situation and things that are not, and things that are sometimes part of it and sometimes not?

9. What are the significant events, trends, people, and influences involved?

10. Could you pool resources with anyone else?

11. Is there a place or person near you that could help you with a problem like this?

12. Is there a place or person anywhere in the world that could help you with a problem like this? Can you go there? Can you contact people there?

13. How do you know that you have, or can obtain, reliable information?

14. Can your "facts" be confirmed or supported by additional sources or means?

15. Are you considering which ideas your information supports, and which ideas it does *not* support?

16. How do you know you are trying hard enough to achieve a current and accurate picture?

17. What might you have missed?

Micro-Strategy 2. Setting objectives

A clear sense of the direction you want to take is important in problem solving. You should develop a specific idea of where you are going, or what you are trying to do. Otherwise, you won't know when you've arrived, or even if you are making progress.

1. What are you trying to do? Do you have more than one objective?

2. What issues are you struggling with? What do you hope to achieve?

3. What exactly do you mean by your answers to questions 1 and 2? Can they be made clearer and more specific?

4. Have you examined your answers carefully for ambiguity, inconsistencies, or contradictions?

5. What are your short-term or immediate aims?

6. What are your longer-term, more distant goals?

7. Does your long-term objective lead to a further objective? Can this objective be broken down into intermediate objectives or sub-goals?

8. What do your goals imply? What tasks do they lead to, within what time frames? What are the steps along the way?

9. What exactly would your proposed new situation look like?

10. What will be your signs of success? How will you decide when you have resolved things?

11. What will be the key signs of success? Which signs will be less important?

12. How successful would you like to be?

13. What measure of success will you be satisfied with?

14. What is the least that *must* be done?

15. What is the most that *can* be done?

16. Are you being realistic about your strengths and weaknesses, or those of others involved, and planning with these strengths and weaknesses in mind?

17. If you can reach only some of your objectives, what are your priorities?

18. Do you have alternate paths of action? If one way is blocked would another be satisfactory?

19. Is this objective really what you want?

Now you may wish to use Micro-Strategy 3, omitting the few questions that duplicate questions you have just considered.

Micro-Strategy 3. Organizing to tackle a problem

Making a good start is half the battle. Disorder usually leads to chaos. Clarify how you are going to operate, now, before the action starts. You may not have time to recover later.

1. What are you trying to do? Where are you trying to go?

2. What seem to be the crucial aspects of this situation? What are the critical points?

3. What will be your signs of success? How will you decide when you have resolved things?

4. Is there anything special or unusual about this situation? Must you be especially cautious? Or can you take advantage of the special or unusual aspects?

5. At what level or from what direction should this problem be approached?

6. What are your targets? How much time do you need? Have you set deadlines? What are your priorities? How soon do you want the situation resolved?

7. What is the least that *must* be done?

8. What is the most that *can* be done?

9. Can a core of difficulty be identified?

10. How complicated does this problem seem to be? How many components, divisions, or levels does it seem to have?

11. Can this problem be broken down into sub-problems that can safely be dealt with individually? Or can the situation be split up into distinct categories, parts, or areas of difficulty? What are these?

12. What are your strengths? How could you use these to respond here?

13. Can you see one point that might be easier than any other to find out about, tackle, or control? Can you do something about this?

14. In how many different ways can you reach your objectives? Which one seems to be the best choice? Which satisfies most of your criteria?

15. Should you consider a smaller range of events, or start with a part of the problem?

16. Should you tackle a larger problem that contains, causes, or lies behind the present problem?

17. Should you take this problem one step at a time and reduce it piece by piece?

18. What seem to be the chief points to decide about or wrestle with?

19. Which areas look as though they'll need the most time, the most energy?

20. Which parts must be kept in harmony with each other?

21. What would be the most effective arrangement of all these pieces?

22. Should you give this solution a trial run before you decide about it?

23. How will you check what progress you're making?

Micro-Strategy 4. Basic fact-finding

Gather the who, which, where, when, how, and why of the situation as a start on your information collecting. Make sure your objectives are clear, or you'll end up with all kinds of useless information. Be clear, too, about what you want to find out.

1. What do you already know?

2. What can you quickly find out?

3. What seems to be happening? What difficulties does this cause? What opportunities does this present?

4. Where is it all taking place?

5. When is it taking place?

6. How is it taking place?

7. How long do the events last? How are they timed?

8. At what rate are things moving?

9. How might this be happening?

10. Who does this? Who is responsible?

11. Who might be causing it?

12. What does the overall situation look like?

13. Which areas seem to be the main trouble spots, or potential trouble spots?

14. What are the components and who are the participants of this problem? How many are there?

15. What are the most critical or noteworthy aspects of this problem? Why?

16. How complicated does this problem seem to be? How many components, divisions, or levels does it seem to have?

17. How has this problem developed?

18. When did this start?

19. How do you know your information is correct and unbiased?

20. Is there anything that you're not sure about or that you don't know?

Micro-Strategy 5. Defining, interpreting, and diagnosing the problem
Look behind the basic facts, the symptoms, and the appearances. Try to interpret clearly and specifically what is going on, and try to find the real source of the difficulty or problem. Are things really what they seem, or what you first thought?

1. What are you trying to figure out? Do you have any good guesses?

2. Why do you see this as a problem? What objectives are not being achieved?

3. What kind of problem is this? What is this problem's

place in the general scheme of things? Does considering this question help to orient you?

4. Is this problem too involved or difficult for you to deal with alone?

5. What are the objectives of the operation, framework, structure, or system that is bothering you?

6. What are the components and who are the participants of this problem? How many are there?

7. How complicated does this problem seem to be? How many components, divisions, or levels does it seem to have?

8. Which part of your problem is most disturbing and why?

9. Is there a core of complexity?

10. Are there any odd coincidences?

11. Can you detect distinct patterns?

12. How do the pieces tie together? What are their inter-relationships? Is anything missing?

13. What kind of structure or pattern is formed by these components and their interrelationships? Do they form a tidy system? Is anything missing?

14. How is this system or situation related, by interconnection or interchange, to outside events, contexts, or environments? Could these relationships be changed? Is anything missing?

15. How might future developments affect this situation?

16. How many interpretations, definitions, or diagnoses can you think of?

17. Can you see contradictions or inconsistencies?

18. Have your "facts" been confirmed or supported by additional sources or means?

19. Is there anything that you're not sure about or that you don't know?

20. Have you checked up on this area, even though most people may feel sure about it?

Micro-Strategy 6. Making a crisis plan

You can't plan for all emergencies, but you can prepare yourself for many crises, especially if you know that the course of action you are about to engage in will have some critical outcomes. Think about these possibilities now, and you may well lessen the impact of an emergency, even if you can't avoid it altogether.

WHAT MUST YOU DEFEND OR RESCUE?
Make sure that basic functions and purposes survive.

FIRST LOOK

    1. What activities, functions, people, relationships, or items must you preserve or rescue?

    2. What people, equipment, services, or actions are required to do this?

    3. How might you satisfy these requirements?

    4. Do you know what information you will need to remain aware of what is happening?

    5. How will you decide what your information or news indicates?

    6. How will you see, predict, or find out about what might happen next?

    7. How will you decide whether or not you should act, and what action you might take?

SECOND LOOK

    1. What gives meaning to your life or your operation? What do you care deeply about? Is there a higher objective or principle that could guide you? Can you use this to find a focus?

    2. Can you in any way reduce the range of issues requiring your immediate attention? What is vital to survival?

    3. Can you tease out, identify, and tackle a central problem or group of problems? What is the crux of the matter?

    4. What are the basic, fundamentally important areas?

    5. What is the most that *can* be done?

    6. What is the least that *must* be done?

HOW MIGHT THIS BE DONE?
Get organized—and fast.

    1. Is there a technique, procedure, theory, principle,

agency, or concept already developed and available that would allow you to deal with this situation speedily and effectively?

2. Is there a skill that you can call upon, either in yourself or someone else, that would help you to deal with this situation speedily and effectively?

3. How will you cope with this emergency and future ones? How will you organize things? What steps will you take?

4. How should your action be organized? What timing is necessary?

5. Which parts will have the greatest impact if they succeed? If they fail? If they are delayed, disorganized, rearranged?

6. Have you covered the things that might become vital if the situation changes? Are your plans flexible?

7. How can you move fast on this?

8. What are the target dates, target amounts, or target positions?

Micro-Strategy 7. What's going wrong here?

Problems are often not what they seem. What looks like a problem may not be one at all. And a problem that seems minor may actually be serious. It always pays to take a close and careful look at what you see as your problem. Solving the wrong problem usually creates more problems.

1. Why do you think something is going wrong?

2. What seem to be the symptoms?

3. Has something changed to cause this feeling of things going wrong? Or, is it the way you are handling things? Or, is there some other cause?

4. Has the situation already changed in a manner that's difficult to recognize? Is the situation different even though it seems the same?

5. Has the situation remained fundamentally the same despite apparent changes?

6. What else is going on? Is it significant? Can you connect your situation with this other thing going on, either by discovering subtle links or by making an innovation?

7. What seem to be the issues or factors involved?

8. Which things are symptoms and which causes? Are some of the things you think are causes really symptoms?
9. Would a single explanation be sufficient, or are several things amiss here, and perhaps presenting a confused picture?
10. Where else could you find information about this situation?
11. What sources that you've never thought of or that you have previously considered and rejected might be available?
12. What might happen next? In the near future? In the long term?
13. What are the different shapes the future might take? What actions might trigger these future events? What information would indicate the direction being taken?

14. Are you considering which ideas your information supports, and which ideas it does *not* support?
15. Are there any odd coincidences?
16. Is there a common thread running through all your problems? That is, are all or many of your difficulties related in some way?
17. Could you find a pattern by altering your viewpoint or changing your expectations of this situation?
18. Could somebody be misleading you? Accidentally? Deliberately?
19. Might you find a pattern by delving into the assumptions, beliefs, concepts, or values with which you are approaching this situation and life in general? Can you examine the context in which you are setting all this?

Micro-Strategy 8. Planning ahead
When we think ahead, we usually do so fragmentarily, covering many levels. Inconsistent or incompatible goals are common. We may have a few small tasks that we know we must accomplish, and we may have a fairly clear idea of some overall strategic goals. But usually we do not have a picture of how everything fits together. The purpose of planning ahead is to close the gaps, to tie it all together so that the details make sense in the light of overall goals, and so that overall goals can be converted into detailed and effective action.

1. What is happening in the short term that you know you have to deal with?
2. What actions will you take to tackle these short-term situations? Make a list of these details.
3. What are these things a part of? Where do they fit? What links can you make?
4. What is going to happen in the long term that you will have to deal with?
5. Can you divide these activities or events into different areas, groups, or types of activities or problems?
6. How are these detailed actions related to your overall objectives? Which larger objective is each detailed action designed to further?

7. What are your overall objectives? What are the steps along the way? What intermediate goals must you reach to achieve these objectives?

8. What activities are required for you to achieve your objectives or your intermediate goals?

9. Can you break these objectives and intermediate goals down into more detailed activity requirements?

10. Can you lay out a flowchart, hierarchy, breakdown, or some other picture of the sub-problems, sub-components, or decisions to be made?

11. Can you lay out a flowchart, hierarchy, or breakdown of the possible outcomes?

12. Which activities are critical to survival? Which activities support your more important goals?

13. What priorities do the various tasks have? Can you rank them in order of importance?

14. What things should interlock?

15. Which activities need careful scheduling or timing?

16. Can you look into the future and see what might thwart your plans?

17. What have you missed? Is there any area you haven't thought about?

18. Can you produce an overall picture of all this and see clearly how everything fits together?

19. Can you develop different routes to your overall objectives, for example, different intermediate goals, so that when one route is blocked another might still be open?

20. How many alternate routes to your goals can you develop?

21. Can you now develop a preferred plan and a couple of backup plans?

Micro-Strategy 9. Having a bright idea

All too often, when we must produce a bright, new idea, we are standing squarely in front of the problem. This is like standing with your nose up against a brick wall and trying to jump over the wall from that position. It is better to stand back and take a run at the wall or even to look for a gate in the wall beside you. To do this with a problem is tricky. You must use imagination in hunting for new perspectives. You *have* to look at the problem in a novel way before you can start to have innovative or unusual ideas. This little strategy is designed to keep your mind poking into out-of-the-way places.

1. What are you trying to do?

2. How many ways can you look at this situation? From what angles? Personal, motivational, technological, social, political, emotional, rational, visual, pictorial, aesthetic, theoretical, technical, financial, organizational, ethical?

3. Where could you find sources of information that would help you to look at the situation in different ways?

4. Who could give you another outlook on this situation?

5. What unusual approach can you take with this problem?

6. Can you split it into different dimensions or aspects?

7. Can you do something unusual with one or more of these aspects?

8. Can this unusual approach be used to provide an unusual solution?

9. Can you take a minor part of the problem and do something unusual with it? How can you exploit this opportunity?

10. Can you describe your objectives in another way? Perhaps rephrasing the objectives, or looking at your goals in a different light, will lead to a different array of ideas for solutions.

11. Who else does something that is similar to what you want to achieve?

12. What else has a form or configuration anything like this?

13. Can you think of processes, ideas, or analogies from the seashore, the farm, your local park, the bird world, the mountains, or the desert that are similar to what you are dealing with?

14. Can you find something to spark ideas, for example, on your kitchen table, on the street, in a department store, in your toolbox, or in a drugstore?

15. Force your mind to generate ideas for this problem from situations involving a comb, a piece of string, a candle, a hinge, a pair of spectacles, a wheel, a can, a zipper, a meteor, a caterpillar, a gate, the sun, an explosion, a river. Select one or two items to work on.

16. Look out the window. Let the first thing you see set your thoughts about the problem on a new path.

17. If you waved a magic wand over this situation, how would you change it, and what ideas does your response give you?

18. What is the most absurd solution you can think of? What is the craziest thing you could do? Does your response give you any sensible ideas?

19. If one of the people involved in this were a Martian, what other issues would emerge and what issues would become less important? What does your response tell you about your problem?

Micro-Strategy 10. Seeking a change of perspective
Figure out what you are trying to do, and where you are currently looking for answers. Then see if you can shift your perspective so that you can look for answers in new places, at new levels, or in a different state of mind. A fresh approach is important if you are to find workable alternatives.

1. What are you trying to do?
2. What will be your signs of success? How will you decide when you have resolved things?
3. Can the problem be split up into distinct categories, parts, or areas of difficulty?
4. Do any of these categories or areas reveal interesting side issues? Can you focus on these? What does the problem look like from that vantage point?
5. How would the French, the Italians, or the Russians deal with this problem?
6. What might a blacksmith, a doctor, or a sailor have to say about it?
7. Can you see one point that might be easier than any other to find out about, tackle, or control? Can you do something about this?
8. What are you assuming about the background against which this difficulty is happening? Are your assumptions valid?
9. Can you change your view of how this situation fits into the larger picture?
10. Is there another place you could start?
11. Is there something engrossing you can do to put this problem out of your mind for a while? If so, perhaps when you return to the problem you'll feel refreshed and see the situation differently.
12. Can you start at the end and work backwards? Can you turn the problem upside down?
13. What other situations can you find in which the principles are similar to the principles in this one?
14. Are you looking at this problem in different ways, on different levels? Have you considered such aspects as organization, aesthetics, personality, timing, information, motivation, effort, production, finance?

15. Does thinking about the preceding list of aspects change the way you see the problem?

16. What psychological or emotional blockages and blind spots in yourself or in others may be involved?

17. Are there any odd coincidences?

18. Who could give you another outlook on this situation?

19. How could you solve this problem in a magical world? Does this solution give you ideas for working on the actual problem?

20. What is the most absurd solution you can think of? What is the craziest thing that could happen? Does this give you any sensible ideas for working on the problem?

21. Can you change the context of your problem?

Micro-Strategy 11. Modeling a situation or a solution

"What would happen if . . . ?" is a valuable question to ask in problem solving. If you have a situation or a solution and you want to see what would happen under different circumstances, a good way to find out without upsetting the actual conditions is to make a model of the idea, process, or procedure. This model can take the form of a drawing, chart, flowchart, physical map or model, set of formulae, or imaginary scene or scenario. The principle is to make things concrete enough that you can play with them and see what they do.

1. Do you have a clear picture of what you are trying to achieve? What state of affairs are you trying to bring about?

2. Can you identify and describe *all* the components and participants in this situation?

3. Can you identify and describe *all* the information pathways?

4. Can you identify and describe *all* the interactions between the parts, showing what happens if and when they interact?

5. Can you identify and describe time scales, rhythms, or flows in activities, or in the way this situation changes shape?

6. What is the importance or priority of each part? Which part affects the greatest number of other parts? Which part has the strongest effects or influence?

7. What decision processes are there in the situation? What controls or influences are there?

8. What uncertainties, unpredictabilities, or instabilities are there?

9. How do the pieces and activities fit together and harmonize, or fail to, in a general movement, rhythm, or operation?

10. Can each part, pathway, function, flow, or rhythm be represented in some way for example, in a chart, graph, flowchart, formula, drawing, scale model, working model, game, or play?

11. Can you build a working model that is a mathematical, physical, or conceptual structure?

12. Which type of modeling seems most appropriate to the kind of situation you have? Which type, for example, handles the situation's complexity or abstraction properly?

13. Can you lay out a hierarchy, flowchart, or breakdown of possible choices and outcomes?

14. How can actual processes, functions, time scales, and activities be represented in the model?

15. How can the structure and workings of the situation, or new proposal, be imitated?

16. How much of your situation and its processes can your model represent?

17. Can you operate your model in different ways and get a feeling for how things might be working in actuality?

18. Does your model clarify fundamental relationships and processes? Are any areas still vague?

19. If there is uncertainty, unpredictability, or instability in the situation, is this properly represented or even recognized? Can you imitate or simulate the condition by using dice, cards, or random-number tables?

20. How far must you test your model before you can accept it as a picture of the real situation? Be ingenious.

21. When you operate the model to simulate the flows, changes, rhythms, and uncertainties of life, does your model respond properly? That is, does it give results comparable to real actions, and does it predict and act in a realistic manner?

22. How closely can your model represent life without being too cumbersome or complicated to operate quickly?
23. If you cannot make your model detailed or complex enough to represent life, are you trying to model the wrong processes or using the wrong type of model?
24. Can the model easily reflect the changes that take place in the world?

Micro-Strategy 12. Finding a pattern
Fitting the pieces of a situation into a pattern requires both imagination and painstaking effort. It's a little like trying to put together a giant's jigsaw puzzle in the fog. Seeing the whole picture is difficult. The questions in this micro-strategy switch you back and forth between the tasks of pulling the pieces together and looking for different ways to view the whole.
1. Are there any odd coincidences?
2. Can you reduce the range of issues you are looking at? Can you find a focus?
3. Is there a common thread running through all the parts of this problem? That is, are all or many of the parts related in some way?
4. Can you tease out, identify, and tackle a central problem, or group of problems?
5. Might you find a pattern by altering your viewpoint or changing your expectations of the situation?
6. What hidden or unstated goals or directions might there be?
7. Could somebody be misleading you? Accidentally? Deliberately?
8. What is the most prominent, intriguing, fruitful, or useful aspect of this situation? Can you use it to find a new angle?
9. Can you start at the end and work backwards? Can you turn the problem upside down?
10. Is there anything here that is so much a part of the accepted way of looking at things that it might not be considered an issue?
11. Are you bringing to this situation an inappropriate or unrealistic set of expectations concerning the outcome, your

capabilities, or the behavior or attitudes of others?

12. Might you find a pattern by delving into the assumptions, beliefs, concepts or values with which you are approaching this situation and life in general? Can you examine the context in which you are setting all this?

13. Can you see decisive patterns in growth or change rates and directions, in components or factors, in their interrelationships?

14. What are the basic items, assumptions, beliefs, or concepts that you are dealing with?

15. What exactly do you mean by the terms you are using, by the viewpoints you are expressing, by the questions you are asking?

16. How could you restate your attitudes, assumptions, or ground rules to reveal any need for clarification, reformulation, or tidying up?

17. Which parts of this problem are objective and verifiable and which are subjective, based on values, taste, opinion or attitude?

18. Could you look at this problem in a way that throws a different light on it? That is, could it be seen as part of another issue? Could the problem be viewed as a chance to straighten out a different problem? Maybe it's an opportunity in disguise.

Micro-Strategy 13. Decision making and selecting from alternatives

Part of problem solving is making decisions. This process must be preceded by careful thought concerning what is required and how it can be achieved. If you don't start out with a clear view of your problem, you may make the right decision on the wrong problem, and thus waste your time, or do worse. Make sure you understand what is going on, and where you wish to go. Then you can decide on how to get there.

1. What is required here? What needs must be satisfied, what conditions met?

2. Must you decide now or can you decide later? If you have a choice, which time would be most advantageous?

3. What will be your signs of success? How will you decide

when a satisfactory decision has been made or when your objectives have been achieved?

4. Which signs of success will be the key ones? Which signs will be less important? What *must* you achieve? What will you be satisfied with?

5. Do you have alternative paths of action? If one way is blocked would another be satisfactory?

6. Are you seriously considering more than one alternative? Or, are you concentrating on the approach that seems to solve the most immediate aspects of the problem, or on the first appealing answer that sprang to mind?

7. Which parts of this problem are objective and verifiable and which are subjective, based on values, taste, opinion, or attitude?

8. For each alternative, have you considered the following elements: areas of accelerating growth; evolutionary, developmental, or historical patterns; interactions between parts, people, factors; personal, technical, social, political, emotional, rational, visual, aesthetic, theoretical, technological, financial, or organizational points; information, attitudes, energy, timing, or production?

9. Who benefits or suffers as a result of each alternative?

10. Have you considered what might happen outside the immediate problem area?

11. Can you identify a core of difficulty?

12. What duration, cost, priority, and potential are associated with the parts of each alternative?

13. How might future developments affect each alternative? Will things remain in their present arrangement?

14. For each alternative, can you list the choice points, decisions, risks, and uncertainties?

15. Which alternatives are more appealing, more effective, more motivating, more economical, faster, or less troublesome than the others?

16. Which alternatives contain the greatest number of new ideas or forms or are the most flexible, adaptive, powerful, simple, or clear?

17. Have you considered what, if any, trade-offs may have to be made in selecting each alternative?

18. What resources are used, what costs incurred, or what danger courted in each solution?

19. Which alternatives consume resources that could be better used elsewhere?

20. Which alternatives consume more resources than are merited by the alternatives, output and value?

21. If each alternative has several possible outcomes, and you cannot decide which would be best, can you decide which alternative would be worst?

Micro-Strategy 14. Building a solution

If you have an idea for resolving a problem and you want to develop it into a full solution, this little strategy should help you explore and elaborate your idea. Follow the ramifications. Pick up the loose ends. Make sure your idea is sound enough to stand as a complete solution.

1. What is required here? What needs must be satisfied, what conditions met?

2. Where are the relevant ideas and information that you have so far? Can you pull them together?

3. Out of this material can you extract what seem to be the central issues?

4. Can you clarify things by arranging the ideas or information around these central issues?

5. What are the important parts, relationships, or outcomes? What are the priorities? What is the crux of the matter?

6. Which leads look as though they'll guide you in the most fruitful direction? Where are the best ideas, explanations, or contributions for your solution likely to be found?

7. How do you think all this fits together? Have you a first guess or a hunch to test out?

8. Can you think of a metaphor or analogy that could get you started on pulling things together?

9. Can you see a simple form in the situation, an underlying process?

10. Is there a pattern you can pick out or invent to explain this?

11. Which parts must be kept in harmony?

12. How many separate parts, subsections, and connections between them should the solution have?

13. How many levels of organization should the solution have? That is, should the solution contain a hierarchy of sub-systems?

14. Which parts could give each other support? Can this mutual benefit be arranged?

15. Which parts might undermine each other? Can this wastefulness be avoided?

16. Consider whether you have covered the following elements of the problem:

—all the parts. Have you missed anything?

—the ways the parts will all fit together, interlock, or interact. Do these parts form a coherent structure, that is, do their interactions, functions, processes, and patterns make sense? Does the whole thing look right?

—the total structure. Is it a coherent pattern? Is it harmonious? What coordinates the structure? What processes hold it together?

—information flows or channels. Communications? Messages? Is information transmitted quickly, clearly, to the right places, and without redundancy?

—decisions, control, organization. How will the parts stay together? How will the situation keep going?

—uncertainty, unpredictability. Have you planned for trouble?

—growth, change, evolution. How will the situation develop or be developed? What are you going to do to promote development?

17. Where should you clarify, elaborate, develop further ideas? What fuzzy areas are left?

18. What decisions still have to be made?

19. Can you list the outstanding tasks in priority sequence?

20. Will anyone resent or resist this solution? Why?

21. Can you think of a better idea with which to tie things together? Can you improve your original concept?

22. How might you achieve deeper insights?

23. Could you take a broader look at the situation?

24. Could your resolution be more extensive?

Micro-Strategy 15. Reconsidering the problem situation

From time to time it can be helpful to look at your view of the problem and ask yourself, "Do I have this all wrong? Could something else be going on here?" If you aren't careful, as you become familiar with a problem situation, you can gradually slip into fixed ways of looking at things. This hinders the development of good solutions. Keep looking for fresh viewpoints.

1. Could the situation be reorganized? Could you see it from different perspectives?

2. Do you have any information at hand that could show that the situation is not what it seems?

3. Is this problem worth solving? If so, what degree of effort seems appropriate?

4. Is there anything that is so much a part of the accepted way of looking at things that it might not be considered an issue?

5. Do you feel that you have grasped what is happening?

6. Do you have any misgivings about your information? If so, examine the uncertain area carefully. Does your examination lead to different interpretations?

7. Who could give you another outlook on this situation?

8. What other things could your interpretation of the situation imply or lead to? Can you find any evidence for this? Does considering this question lead to new avenues of inquiry?

9. What can be inferred from this situation? What does it imply? What does the situation lead to?

10. How is this situation developing? What is its history? What could its future be? How many different ways could it develop in the future?

11. Does this raise deeper issues?

12. Are things really more complicated than this, or simpler?

13. What is puzzling you?

14. Should you tackle a larger problem that contains, causes, or lies behind the present problem?

15. Are you trying to tease out the truth, or to construct what you would like to find?

16. How can you solve this problem most advantageously?
17. Is this situation part of a larger problem?
18. Do you have to look beyond the present range of events to find the causes, or the motivating or controlling forces?
19. What hidden or unstated goals or directions might there be?
20. Are you looking at the problem upside down?

Micro-Strategy 16. Checking out your solution, I
In this and the next two micro-strategies, the idea is to do your best to destroy your solution. Sounds ridiculous? Well, it isn't. If your solution is any good, no amount of prodding, poking, and investigating will do it any harm. Maybe you will find some loose ends to clean up and will improve the solution. If the solution is bad, better to find out now and save yourself embarrassment or disaster later.

1. Is your proposal doomed from the start?
2. Is this solution what you really want? Is it really what is needed?
3. What are the greatest risks? What are the greatest challenges? Can you handle them?
4. Can you find loose ends? What are you going to do about them?
5. Is any part of your proposal inconsistent with or at odds with another part?
6. Does your proposal contain hidden contradictions or inconsistencies?
7. Are you seriously considering more than one solution? Or, have you rushed for the solution that seems to solve the most immediate aspects of the problem, or for the first appealing answer that sprang to mind?
8. Is your research thorough?
9. Is the solution really as imaginative as you think?
10. Is the solution really as comprehensive as you think?
11. Are you resisting the possibility that you may have to throw it all out and start again?
12. Are there other ideas that come close to your idea, or that have been put into effect to handle your concerns?
13. How does your idea measure up to these other ideas?

14. Are there other ideas that reflect the opposite or different conclusions from the ones that your idea reflects?

15. What can you deduce from this?

16. In what ways have others gone further than you? How? Why?

17. Will your idea solve the problem, transfer it somewhere else, or hide it?

18. How do you plan to make your solution operate?

19. Have you planned the implementation in detail?

20. What actions and stages are required? How will you prevent these from becoming unsynchronized?

Micro-Strategy 17. Checking out your solution, II
For the rationale behind this micro-strategy, read the introduction to Micro-Strategy 16.

1. Will your solution have effects elsewhere?

2. Could your solution be moving on a collision course with anything else?

3. What effects might other things have on your solution?

4. What effects might the solution have on other things?

5. Why might this happen and when?

6. What might be the results?

7. How would these effects be handled?

8. Have you considered what, if any, trade-offs may have to be made in selecting from the alternative solutions you have developed?

9. If each of your solutions has several possible outcomes, and you cannot decide which solution would be best, can you decide which solution would be worst and eliminate that one?

10. What resources are used, what costs incurred, or what danger courted by each alternative solution?

11. Will anyone develop or benefit as a result from this situation?

12. Will anyone suffer?

13. What might happen outside the immediate problem area?

14. What duration, cost, priority, and potential does each part of your proposal have?

15. How might future developments affect this situation?

16. When you take each part of the solution and consider its future, do things remain in the same arrangement?

17. If you can see anything that might go wrong, can you think of a way of handling it?

18. Can you foresee disasters for your solution? How would you avoid such disasters?

Micro-Strategy 18. Checking out your solution, III

For the rationale behind this micro-strategy, read the introduction to Micro-Strategy 16.

1. What are the strong points of the solution? How much do they contribute to the problem area?

2. Is the solution inventive? Does it encourage diversity, richness, new ideas, forms, structures, or concepts?

3. Is the solution flexible? Does it allow quick changes of direction and configuration?

4. Is the solution adaptive? Does it allow smooth handling of changes in internal and external circumstances?

5. Can you cope with complexity, using this solution?

6. Can you hold to a steady course, resisting disruption, if you use this solution?

7. Does the solution make things simpler? Does it make things clearer?

8. What are the weak points in this proposal?

9. Is this a stop-gap solution, or is it grounded in an overall strategy?

10. What is your proposal unprepared for?

11. Will your proposal cause significant changes? If so, will the changes be toward growth or decline?

12. Does anything about your proposal bother you? It is better to find the flaws before implementation rather than after.

13. Does your proposal use resources that would be better spent elsewhere?

14. Does the outcome or value of your proposal justify the resources it uses?

15. Are any of your assumptions erroneous? Check all the things you think are obvious. Are they?

16. What decisions must be made?

17. For each point at which a decision is to be made, what are the risks and uncertainties?

18. How do the decision points and risks differ with each alternative?

19. Which alternative contains the most hazards?

Micro-Strategy 19. Organizing to implement a solution

Many a good idea fails when it's turned into a solution and put into effect. Converting your solution into a successful answer to your problem requires planning and monitoring, activities that can be problems in themselves. Treat these problems with care.

1. What are you trying to do?

2. What seem to be the main features of this situation? What seem to be the crucial points?

3. What are the components and who are the participants of your new situation? Have you specified these?

4. What seem to be the chief points you must wrestle with or make decisions about?

5. Should you give this proposal a trial run before installing a full-scale solution?

6. Which areas look as though they'll need the most time, the most energy?

7. Can all areas be handled? If not, which ones should you concentrate on?

8. Which activities need careful scheduling or timing? What is the best scheduling or timing of these?

9. Which parts of the solution will have the greatest impact if they succeed? If they fail? If they are delayed, disorganized, or rearranged?

10. How should action be organized? How should the action be timed?

11. Is a team of people required to carry out the solution? Who will they be? What skills, knowledge, or attitudes should they have? What training will the team require?

12. How must the tasks be arranged and sequenced for best effect? Can this be done?

13. Which parts must be kept in harmony?

14. Which parts could give each other support? Can this mutual benefit be arranged?

15. Which parts might undermine each other? Can this wastefulness be avoided?

16. What are your targets? How much time do you need? Have you set deadlines? What are your priorities?

17. Must anything else happen to make your solution possible? What can you do to make sure it does happen?

18. How will you keep track of progress?

19. Can you put alternate plans and procedures into effect if things start to go wrong?

20. How will you keep watch for the unanticipated?

21. Have you a plan for assessing the solution after it has been carried out?

22. Does everyone who will be affected by the solution understand and accept the possible changes?

Micro-Strategy 20. Reviewing your approach or strategy
Keep an eye on your performance. It's easy to fall into sloppy habits as you become familiar with a situation. This happens so gradually that not noticing it is almost forgivable. From time to time, take a look at how you are doing—a close and honest look.

1. Are you achieving your overall objectives?

2. Should you speed up or slow down?

3. Are you going into the problem in sufficient depth?

4. Are you dithering around? Could your work be more concentrated?

5. Are you working in the areas that look as though they'll provide the biggest effects or contribution?

6. Are you putting first things first?

7. Is anything you are doing or contemplating doing trivial or superficial?

8. How might you be running into difficulties? By attempting too much, by delaying, by avoiding difficulties? By being unrealistic, by oversimplifying, or by taking action that is inappropriate to the day-to-day, personal, business, or political realities? By being uncoordinated, impractical, overcomplicated?

9. Is there a more adventurous, bolder, or more inspired way of doing this?

10. Are you overdoing it? Is your approach too cumbersome or complicated?

11. Is anything slipping? Organization, motivation, timing, imagination, judgment, critical review?

12. Can you do less in any area?

13. Could a redirection of effort enable you to make more progress?

14. Do you need a boost for your spirits? Do you need your strength restored? Could friends help?

15. Are you taking on too much? Are you being erratic or panicking because of stress or sudden change?

16. Do you keep changing direction? If so, is it because you are losing your grip on the situation?

17. Are you keeping a clear overall view of the situation? Can you spot trouble before it arrives?

18. Have you been behaving flexibly, imaginatively, and coherently? Can you get a second opinion from someone?

19. Have you changed your view of the situation considerably? Must you now change your approach?

20. Is your approach really suitable? Are your techniques appropriate? Are you being too precise, or too slapdash?

21. Do you really need help in handling this situation?

22. Are you turning a blind eye to anything?

23. Are you in any way causing the difficulties you are faced with?

24. Can you see ways in which you might improve your problem-solving behavior?

Micro-Strategy 21. Reassessing the immediate situation

Situations change. That's the way life is. Sometimes situations change and don't show it on the surface. Sometimes they change on the surface, but underneath nothing is different. Finding out what is changing and what to do about it, if anything, can help you to stay in control of your problem situation.

1. Are you achieving the overall objectives?

2. Where do you stand with this project?

3. Are new patterns appearing? If so, what do they look like?

4. Should you implement your crisis plan? Do you have a crisis plan? If not, use Micro-Strategy 6 to devise one.

5. Does it look as though the situation is changing or about to change?

6. Has the situation already changed in a manner that's hard to recognize?

7. Has the situation remained fundamentally the same despite apparent changes?

8. What new patterns of events might emerge?

9. How could current trends be reinterpreted? What changes might these reinterpretations bring about?

10. What could you do to be ready for this?

11. Can you locate the source of any unpredictability, threat, or competition?

12. Who or what might be causing any unpredictability? Now? In the future?

13. Is there anything else going on that may soon affect your situation? Do you see surprises on the way?

14. Is anything falling behind? Is anything getting out of step? If so, what will the effect be? What will you do about it?

15. If you can foresee something that might go wrong, how will you handle it, either to prevent it going wrong or to deal with it afterwards?

16. Does it look as though the future of this situation will differ considerably from the past?

17. Have you gained a new perspective? Does the new viewpoint make a new solution or new approach look possible?

18. Are there any new problems to be solved? If so, how will you organize the solving of them?

19. Should you reorganize or reschedule part of the current effort? Should you change priorities, expand, contract?

Micro-Strategy 22. Staying organized

When complexity and pressure build up, it's easy to become disorganized. Keep in mind your objectives, the key issues, and your plan for the approach. Don't lose your way in the maze of details and side issues. Remind yourself, from time to time, where you are headed.

1. Where are you trying to go?

2. What are the rough outlines of the situation?

3. What are the main pieces of your plan, and where do they fit?

4. What are you going to do next? Why? Where does this action fit in the overall plan and/or the sub-problem?

5. Do any parts of the problem overlap? What are you doing to keep this clear?

6. Are you looking at things on different levels or from different viewpoints, without confusing these levels or viewpoints?

7. Are you changing course or tactics with insufficient justification, or too frequently?

8. Are you moving inflexibly, following a fixed pattern?

9. What tasks remain to be done? What tasks may you have missed?

10. Are you keeping a note of possible new ideas, directions, concerns, or dangers?

11. Have you a plan for staying organized through disruption or interruption, be it voluntary or involuntary? How will you keep track of where you were and what you were thinking when you were interrupted?

12. Could you handle this problem more effectively, more competently? Could you take more telling action?

13. Is anything slipping, for example, organization, motivation, timing, imagination, judgment, critical review?

14. Is your solution likely to be moving on a collision course with anything else?

15. Is there a central idea or unifying theme that enables you to keep track of what you are trying to do and to keep your project on the rails?

16. Should you reorganize your efforts for better effect?

17. Are you keeping in mind your reason for solving this problem, or are you being diverted from the main issues?

Micro-Strategy 23. Avoiding a crisis by attacking something concrete

One way to avoid crisis is to get organized in advance. While there is time, find the likely problem areas. You can do this by first narrowing your focus to one area, and then extending your actions over an ever larger portion of the problem situation. In addition, read the remarks about crisis in the introduction to Strategy 7.

1. Do you know what information you need in order to remain aware of what is happening?

2. How will you see, predict, or find out the things that might happen next?

3. How will you decide what your information or news indicates?

4. How will you decide whether you should act, and what action to take?

5. Can you tease out the apparent components and partici-

pants in this situation? How many are there and what or who are they?

6. How is each component or participant related to or affecting the others?

7. Can you identify and describe time scales, rhythms, or flows in activities or in the way this situation changes shape?

8. What uncertainties, unpredictabilities or instabilities are there?

9. Can you arrange the components and interrelationships in order of importance? Which part affects the greatest number of other parts? Which part has the strongest effects or influence?

10. How do the pieces and activities fit together and harmonize, or fail to, in a single movement, rhythm, or operation?

11. Can you reduce the range of issues requiring your immediate attention? Are there fundamentally important activities? What is vital to survival?

12. What gives meaning to your life or operation? What do you care deeply about? Is there a higher objective or principle that could guide you? Can you use this as a focal point?

13. Can you quickly assess the difficulties for their impact on your survival, the people most important to you, your principles or ideals, your future, your operating or living conditions? Can you narrow the situation somewhat, for the moment, by excluding problems in which, for instance, the first two factors are not *vital*? Perhaps you already have a set of priorities with which to do this.

14. Can you identify the things that you cannot immediately do anything about, the things that are not under your control or influence? If so, can you leave these things for now? (Not for ever!)

15. Is there something worrisome, troublesome, or threatening that you can quickly get out of the way?

16. Can the problem be broken down into categories, parts, or areas of difficulty?

17. Which areas look as though they'll need the most time, the most energy?

18. Can all areas be handled? If not, which ones should you concentrate on?

19. Have you covered everything that might become vital if things change? Are your plans flexible?

20. Which activities need careful scheduling or timing? What is the best scheduling and timing for these activities?

21. Which activities are the most uncertain or raise the most questions?

22. Which parts will have the greatest impact if they succeed? If they fail? If they are delayed, disorganized, rearranged?

23. Can you tease out, identify, and tackle a central problem or group of problems?

24. Can you pull out one problem to focus on, and get started?

Having narrowed the range of difficulties, you may wish to work on the first problem, and then gradually broaden your scope, moving outward from the most crucial problems to less critical ones, in the way that concentric ripples move outward in a pool. As you gain more control over your situation, reduce the seriousness of your difficulties, and achieve more time, you will be able to take a broader perspective and perhaps reassess problems already dealt with. Better solutions may start appearing possible or advisable.

Micro-Strategy 24. Taking stock

When you're working on a problem, you should pause from time to time to look at how you and your project are doing. Are you making the progress you'd hoped to? Have things changed much? Get a clear and honest overview of what is going on, and see what, if anything, should be done about it.

1. Are you achieving your overall objectives?

2. Have your actions had the required effects? If not, why did they fail? How long did things survive and why?

3. Does the reason for failure present you with insights or new perspectives?

4. If your actions were a success, can you do still more?

5. Have your actions or their effects presented new opportunities? If so, what can be done to exploit these?

6. Were your actions really effective, or are appearances deceiving you?

7. Did something just happen or change? If so, will it affect the situation? Where does the event or change fit? What could be done about it?

8. Should you implement your crisis plan? Do you have a crisis plan? If not, use Micro-Strategy 6 to devise one.

9. What would be a surprising way the situation could change?

10. Imagine that the situation, events, or participants are conspiring to surprise you. What would be your weakest spot? What might happen?

11. What could you do to be ready for this?

12. What else is going on? Is it significant? Can you connect your situation with this other thing going on, either by discovering subtle links or by making an innovation?

13. What would happen if the problem situation suddenly deteriorated or if it suddenly improved?

14. If you can see anything that might go wrong, can you think of a way of handling it or preventing it?

15. Have you gained new perspectives? Does one of these viewpoints indicate that a new solution or a new approach is possible?

16. Do any new problems need to be solved? If so, how will you organize this?

17. Should you reorganize or reschedule any part of the current effort? Should you change priorities, expand, contract?

18. Did you do this in the most effective way? Did you take the best course of action?

19. Did you try to cut out activities that did not contribute directly to the overall objectives? Did you concentrate on the activities that did contribute?

20. Can you improve the way you tackle problems so that you can devise better solutions in the future?

Micro-Strategy 25. Reorienting to a new perception of a situation

From time to time you may look at your problem and see it in a new light. Things may have become better or worse, or may have changed entirely. When this happens, you may need to change some things. This micro-strategy should help you to establish what is different, and what should change as a result.

1. What seem to be the components of this new situation?
2. Who is involved?
3. What new facts or information do you have?
4. How have relationships changed? What new interactions are there?
5. What functions are different?
6. How has the overall situation, framework, or system changed? How is the total thing different?
7. Has the relationship between the situation and the world around it changed?
8. How have the dynamics of the situation changed? What's going on now? What new patterns or rhythms are there?
9. What is required to psychologically reorient yourself? What do you have to adjust to?
10. What attitudes must change? In yourself? In others?
11. What opinions must change? In yourself? In others?
12. How will your wishes and objectives be modified?
13. What concepts, ideas, frameworks, functions, or interactions should be modified?
14. What actions that are now under way must change?
15. What planned actions must change?
16. What new work, actions, plans, or problems must you deal with?
17. Has your perception of the time available or the situation's duration changed?
18. Have any deadlines changed?
19. What new opportunities are there?
20. How might you take advantage of this?

Now you may wish to turn to Micro-Strategy 3, "Organizing to tackle a problem," or to Micro-Strategy 8, "Planning ahead."

Micro-Strategy 26. For a complicated situation
Often, complicated situations seem more so because we do not pay sufficient attention to interactions and patterns of events.

One method of sorting out the complications is to find out what influences what else and in what way, and how the influences contribute to an overall pattern or flow. Even disorder has patterns. Examining how the interactions within a situation contribute to the overall system is just as important as examining the details.

1. Can you tease out the apparent components and participants of this situation? How many are there and what or who are they?

2. How is each component or participant related to or affecting the others?

3. Which interrelationships are close and strong? Which are loose and weak?

4. Which interrelationships are unchanging? Which do or could change, by fluctuating or by being modified?

5. Is the nature of each interrelationship clear, or is it unknown in some cases, or hard to fathom?

6. Can you identify and describe the information pathways?

7. Can you identify and describe time scales, rhythms, or flows in activities, or in the way this situation changes shape?

8. What decision processes, controls, influences, and organization are involved?

9. What uncertainties, unpredictabilities, or instabilities are there?

10. Can you arrange the components and interrelationships in order of importance? Which one affects the greatest number of other parts? Which part has the strongest effects or influence?

11. Can you produce a hierarchic layout, a diagram, or a flowchart of these parts and interactions?

12. Can you see other patterns, arrangements, or categories that could be made with these pieces?

13. How do the pieces and activities fit together in these other patterns and harmonize, or fail to, in a single movement, rhythm, or operation?

14. Can you examine these other patterns using questions 2 through 11?

15. Which arrangement offers the best picture, explanation, model, or definition of the problem?

16. Can you now review the importance or priority of the various parts and break out the sub-problems to be solved?

17. Can you now solve these sub-problems by finding an approach for each one in the micro-strategies or in Section 6?

18. Can you assemble your sub-problem solutions to form a coherent, overall solution?

19. If not, perhaps one sub-problem solution offers the key to the overall difficulty. Can you use one of these solutions as a focal point?

20. How do the parts of your overall situation fit together? Can you examine this pattern using questions 2 through 11?

21. If some of the parts do not quite fit, how can you resolve this? Must you rework solutions for a sub-problem or two, or has the whole effort been misdirected?

22. Now that you know more about the overall pattern and its parts, can you see new perspectives, or gain a clearer picture of the problem? Does the problem look different from before?

23. If so, can you improve your solution, or can you produce a different and better solution?

Micro-Strategy 27. Tackling an unpredictable situation

Two activities, performed either alternately or in parallel, will help you control an unpredictable situation. First, you should make sure basic functions are protected. Taking this precaution will win you time to do the second activity, which is to probe the reasons for the unpredictability or uncertainty. As you begin to see the situation more clearly, you can improve your emergency plans and make further efforts to resolve the problem.

FIRST LOOK: PRESERVING THE BASICS

1. What activities, functions, people, items, or relationships must you preserve or rescue?

2. What is required in order to do this?

3. How might you accomplish this?

SECOND LOOK: WHAT'S HAPPENING?

1. Can you tease out the apparent components, parts, and participants in this situation? How many are there and what or who are they?

2. How is each one related to or affecting the others?

3. Can you identify and describe time scales, rhythms, or flows in activities, or in the way this situation changes shape?

4. What uncertainties, unpredictabilities, or instabilities are there?

5. Can you arrange the components and interrelationships in order of importance? Which part affects the greatest number of other parts? Which part has the strongest effects or influence?

6. How do the pieces and activities fit together and harmonize, or fail to, in a single movement, rhythm, or operation?

7. Can you reduce the range of issues requiring your immediate attention? Are there fundamentally important activities? What is vital to survival?

8. How can you find out about the unpredictability, uncertainty, or threat? Is there someone you can talk to about it? Is there a place you can look or something you can read, remember, or see that contains information?

9. Can you find the source of the unpredictability?

10. From where and from how many sources is the unpredictability coming?

11. Can you isolate the unpredictable part of the situation and keep clear of it, or tackle it, or minimize its impact?

THIRD LOOK: SEARCH FOR PATTERNS, CLUES, ANSWERS

1. Are there any strange coincidences?

2. Can you see decisive patterns in growth or change rates and directions, in components or factors, or in their interrelationships?

3. Can you tease out, identify, and tackle a central problem, or group of problems?

4. Might you find a pattern by altering your viewpoint or changing your expectations of this situation?

5. What hidden or unstated goals or directions might there be?

6. Could someone be misleading you? Deliberately? Accidentally?

7. Can you start at the end and work backwards? Can you turn the problem upside down?

8. Is there anything that is so much a part of the accepted way of looking at things that it cannot be considered an issue?

When you've gained a clearer picture of the situation, return to Section 6 to select an approach that's suitable for the situation as you now see it.

Micro-Strategy 28. For a fuzzy or confusing situation

The major effort in fuzzy and confusing situations goes into clarification. Clearing up the confusion requires finding out what is going on and what the events signify. It means pondering the ideas and categories involved. In addition, it means finding out what other people are thinking and why, and noting your own perceptions and thoughts. Make sure you pin the situation down and ascertain why it is confusing.

1. Why do you think you have a problem? What seem to be the symptoms?

2. What seems to be happening? What difficulties does this cause? What opportunities does this present?

3. Where are the areas of confusion, fuzziness, or difficulty or where do they seem likely to be found?

4. What do you already know about this situation? What could you quickly find out?

5. Is there anything that you're not sure about or that you don't know?

6. What bits and pieces do you think are involved in this problem? Which ones are important?

7. How complex does this problem seem to be? Can you break it up into smaller parts and then deal with the parts separately to avoid being overwhelmed by the details?

8. What are the most critical or noteworthy aspects of this problem? Why?

9. Can a core of difficulty be identified?

10. Which part of your problem is most disturbing and why?

11. Where else could you find information about this problem?

12. How is this situation developing? What is its history? What could its future be? How many different ways could it develop in the future?

13. How do the components and participants of this problem seem to be tied together? What are their interrelationships? Is anything missing?

14. What can be inferred from what you have learned so far? Where might this lead?

15. Does this raise any deeper issues?

16. What do you understand by the terms, concepts, or ideas that you are dealing with, by the viewpoints that you are expressing, by the questions you are asking?

17. Are you confusing any categories or types of things, mixing things that don't belong together in your scheme? Apples and oranges, for example, are sometimes different (one is citrus, the other not) and sometimes the same (both are fruit and grow on trees).

18. Are you setting out with a wrong idea of what is, or should be, going on?

19. What hidden or unstated goals or directions might there be?

20. Is dealing with the situation primarily a matter of getting organized, of making plans, of establishing priorities?

21. Should you seek information, find out where everything fits, or weigh, sift, assess, test, or diagnose?

22. Should you invent something new, or produce a new plan or idea?

23. Can you see decisive patterns in growth or change rates and directions, in components or factors, or in their interrelationships?

24. Is there a common thread running through all your problems? That is, are all or many of your difficulties related in some way?

25. Might you find a pattern by altering your viewpoint or

changing your expectations of the future or of this situation?

Micro-Strategy 29. Consolidating
The more effort a problem demands, the more likely will be your need to stop from time to time to pull together your work and organize it, or simplify it. It's bad enough having a problem. It's a lot worse if you lose control of your solution process. If you're starting to feel weighed down, condense and simplify before your situation becomes more complicated than the problem you are trying to solve.

1. Have you gathered all your information and ideas, or have you a note recording where they can be located?
2. Have you a record or an indication of all the things you have been working on, or thinking about, or achieving, or planning to achieve?
3. Can you divide the material into categories, arranging them, for example, by priority, type, or progress made; or separating them into such classes as information, ideas, plans, and people; or making some other breakdown?
4. Can you map out a brief outline, chart, sketch, or breakdown of these categories, including their contents, or where their contents could be found?
5. Can you simplify this breakdown, for example, by making some of the categories into sub-categories and so producing an easily handled hierarchic scheme?
6. Can you produce this outline in a form that is easy to juggle and in which you can reorganize the sequences, priorities, and relationships of the categories and their contents on pieces of card, wall charts, or some other means?
7. Would any other means of arrangement or condensation be useful? Graphs, theories, or formulae, for instance, or simply picking out central themes or ideas.
8. Can you select a focal point or central issue around which you can organize everything?
9. Can you arrange all the things you have done or have left to do into a pattern around this focal point?
10. What does this pattern indicate to you? Are there gaps?

Is there anything unnecessary?

11. Can you now tell whether selecting a different focal point would enable you to better organize your information and ideas?

12. Does considering these questions offer you any new perspectives, new ideas, or new opportunities? If so, how can you take advantage of these?

13. Do you want to modify any of your objectives?

14. Can you now produce an overall picture that includes all your concerns, and redevelop your list of tasks, targets, priorities, and implementation plans?

15. Does this arrangement make the best use of your talents, time, and effort? If not, how could you make the arrangement fit you better and yet still fit your overall objectives?

STRATEGIES

Straightforward

In a straightforward situation, the prime requirements are a methodical yet imaginative approach. Even an uncomplicated situation offers the opportunity for contriving a clever and original solution. Take care to organize yourself well, and you'll have a greater opportunity to think things out in a new way. The following strategy contains a procedure to take you all the way from specifying your task to carefully examining your solution and its results.

After some section headings, micro-strategy numbers appear in parentheses. The micro-strategies referred to are suggestions for use, as a whole or in part, if you wish to expand the section. Using the micro-strategies in this way will enable you to adjust the emphasis of your strategy somewhat, depending on your circumstances and the size of the problem. For a fast route through the strategy, use only the questions marked with an asterisk.

For protection against frequent interruption, at intervals make a note of your position and ideas so that you won't forget them. The strategies are divided into segments to provide stopping points.

Outline of tasks
1. Get started.
2. Set objectives.
3. Clarify the problem.
4. Seek imaginative ideas.
5. Construct solutions out of these ideas.
6. Make implementation plans.

7. Assess and improve your solution.
8. Follow up and assess your approach.

1. Get started.

Begin by clarifying what you are trying to achieve.

* What seems to be happening? What difficulties does this cause? What opportunities does this present?
  What is puzzling you?
* What seem to be the significant areas?
  What is this problem's place in the general scheme of things?
  What operating principles are involved?
* What are you trying to figure out?

Is there anything special or unusual about this operation or

HOOT SAYS:

FOR A STRAIGHTFORWARD SITUATION

1. LOOK HARD.
2. THINK IMAGINATIVELY.
3. PLAN INDUSTRIOUSLY.
4. REVIEW CRITICALLY.
5. ACT QUICKLY AND FIRMLY.
6. REVIEW THOROUGHLY.

situation? Must you be especially cautious? Or can you take
advantage of the special qualities?
* What might be the best way to approach this kind of prob-
    lem?
* Should an interim solution be prepared, pending a more thor-
    ough investigation?
    How must the different tasks be arranged and sequenced for
    best effect? Can it be done?
    How will you know when you have solved the problem? How
    will you tell if you are falling behind or headed for failure?

2. Set objectives.
Make sure you know which direction you are heading in (Mi-
cro-Strategy 2).
* What are your short-term goals?
* What are your long-term goals?
    What will be your signs of success? How will you decide
    when you have resolved things?
    When do you want to finish?
    If you can reach only some of the things you want to reach,
    what are your priorities?

3. Clarify the problem.
Figure out what the real issues are. Don't set off with only a
vague and hasty perception of the problem (Micro-Strategy 4).
* What does the overall situation look like?
* Why do you see this as a problem? What objectives are not
    being achieved?
* What do you already know?
* What could you quickly find out?
    What are the components and who are the participants of this
    problem? How many are there?
* What are the most critical or noteworthy aspects of this prob-
    lem? Why?

* How complicated does this problem seem to be? How many
    components, divisions, or levels does it seem to have?
    Does this raise any deeper issues?
    What is being done? What action is being taken in and

around the problem area?
* Why does it all seem to be happening?
  How is it taking place?
* What seem to be the chief points to decide about or wrestle
  with?
  Is there any lasting pattern? Does any relationship, value,
  framework, or process endure?

* What might you have missed?
  What has been the development path of this? When did it
  start?
* Can you detect growth, change, decay, or evolutionary patterns?
* Has this problem had serious effects in other areas? What are
  these? What action has been taken in response?

If you look at the past, does it shed light on potential problems or developments? What else might go wrong, or go right?

Are there any parts that look like difficulties but may not actually be difficulties, or vice versa?

Are you considering which ideas your information supports, and which ideas it does *not* support?

* Are you certain that *this* is the real problem? Are you sure that the problem is what it seems to be?

* Have you considered what might be happening outside the immediate problem area?

What else might be affected—or be an influence?

How do you know your information is correct and unbiased?

Is there anything that you're not sure about or that you don't know?

Who could give you another outlook on this situation?

* Can you detect any distinct patterns?

Are there any strange coincidences?

Can you find some little thing out of joint, some small inconsistency in an otherwise coherent situation? If so, what does this mean? Does this affect your picture of the situation?

* Can you think of another explanation of all this?

* Do all these pieces fit together in a coherent structure, pattern, or explanation? Does the whole thing make sense?

4. Seek imaginative ideas.

Try to move your mind in new channels. Break out of the immediate confines of the problem and look for new ways of seeing things (Micro-Strategies 9 and 10).

* What is the most prominent, intriguing, fruitful, or useful aspect of the problem? Can you use this aspect to find a new angle?

What indirect or unusual approach could you take with your difficulty? What unexpected angles could you try?

* How might the French, the Italians, or the Russians deal with this problem?

Can you put together some hitherto separate parts of your problem?
* Can you change your approach to the situation? For example, if you are facing traffic problems, would it help to think of designing a new kind of car, or a new type of motive power, or drive system? Alternatively, would it help to think about new types of transportation or city design? Can you take both broader and more detailed views?

* How can you modify the scope or boundaries of this problem? How can you expand the problem or contract it? How might that help?
Could this problem be made a part of another system or situation? Can you achieve the same objectives by taking a different route?
* Exaggerate the effects or characteristics of one part of your problem. What ideas does this suggest?
* Think of other ways that some parts could be arranged or could interact.
How could you solve this problem in a magical world? Does this solution give you ideas about how things could be made to work in actuality?

* If these things were taking place in another country, would the problem be significantly different? What ideas does this question provoke?
* Look out your window. Let the first thing you see set your thoughts on a new path of thinking about the problem.
Put yourself in the roles of various participants in this problem. How would you feel about it?
* Toward what goal are you trying to feel your way?
Which bits and pieces are the most important?

* What seem to be the most important parts of this situation? What are the vital points? What is the heart of the matter?
* How can you tie these parts together? What other route could you take toward grasping the situation?
Can you think of a metaphor or analogy that could start you pulling everything together?

* Should you take the problem a step at a time and reduce the problem stage by stage? Can you break the problem down into broad categories and deal with these sections separately, to avoid being overwhelmed by the details?

5. Construct solutions out of these ideas.
Take any potentially fruitful ideas you have, and work them into properly structured solutions. Explore the ins and outs (Micro-Strategies 11, 8, 14, and 13).
* What or who will be the components or participants of your new situation? Have you specified these?
* What seem to be the chief points to decide about or wrestle with?
  What areas are there? Can you handle them all? If not, which ones should you concentrate on?

* Which areas look as though they'll need the most time, the most energy?
  Which activities need careful scheduling or timing? What would be the best scheduling and timing of them?
  Which parts will have the greatest impact if they succeed? If they fail? If they are delayed, disorganized, rearranged?
* Which parts must be kept in harmony with each other?
  Which parts could give each other support? Can this mutual benefit be arranged?

  In what political, organizational, ideological, or policy-oriented context will your solution be set? How will your solution fit into it?
* Will you be able to put alternate plans and procedures into effect if things start to go wrong?
  Have you made specific plans for dealing with uncertainty or instabilities?
* Must anything else happen to make your solution possible? What can you do to make sure it happens?
  What do you need in the way of people's time, materials, equipment, energy, coordination?

* Can you produce a flowchart or decision tree or lay out a hi-

erarchy or breakdown of possible choices and outcomes?
* What decisions must be made?
* Can you build a working model of your situation that is a mathematical, physical, or philosophical structure?
   What kind of modeling seems most appropriate to your situation? That is, what kind of modeling handles the situation's complexity or abstraction properly?

* How closely can your model represent life without being too cumbersome or complicated to operate quickly and simply?
   Does your model clarify fundamental relationships and processes? Are any areas still vague?
   Is any basic uncertainty or variability in the situation you are modeling being hidden by the more concrete and quantifiable aspects?
   How far can you test your model before accepting it as a picture of the real situation?

6. Make implementation plans.
Detail your plan for carrying out your solution. How will you put the plan into effect and keep it operative?
* How do you plan to make your solution operate?
* Should you make a trial run before installing a full-scale solution?
   Can you put your new idea in motion alongside the old situation to compare the two, to test the new idea, or to phase the new idea in gradually?
   What actions and stages are required? How will you prevent these from becoming unsynchronized?
   What will you do to make sure the separate parts of the project interlink smoothly?
* Have you a plan for assessing the solution's success?
   Does everyone affected understand and accept the changes that might occur?
* How will you keep track of progress?
   How will you keep an eye open for the unanticipated?
   If you can see anything that might go wrong, have you thought of a way of handling it?

7. Assess and improve your solution.

Now poke holes in your solution and try to make it into a superior one (Micro-Strategies 15, 16, 17, and 18).

 Is this solution what you really want? Is it really what is needed?
* Does it make a coherent whole, or pattern, or explanation? Does it hang together properly?
* Can you find loose ends? What are you going to do about them?
 Could you take a broader outlook? Are you looking at the situation from too narrow a perspective?
* Are things actually more complicated than this, or simpler?
* Are you seriously considering more than one solution, or have you rushed for the one that seems to solve the most immediate aspects of the problem, or for the first appealing answer that sprang to mind?

 Is anything within this solution at odds with itself?
 Do any of the objectives or procedures of the solution conflict with each other?
 Are you avoiding the alternative of throwing it all out and starting again?
 Will the solution have effects elsewhere?
* Is it moving on a collision course with anything else?
 How might it be affected by something else connected with it?
 How might it affect something else connected with it?

* Have you considered what, if any, trade-offs may have to be made in selecting each alternative?
* What resources are used, what costs incurred, or what danger courted, by each alternative solution?
* Can you find a way to make the solution more effective? More powerful? More significant?
* Can you find a way to make the solution simpler? Is there a simpler answer than this?
 Can you find a way to make the solution move more quickly?
* Can you find a way to make it more flexible?

Can you find a way to make the solution require less energy, attention, or maintenance?

* Can you find a way to make the solution do more with the same input?

Could the solution effect more widespread or comprehensive benefits? What would be required to make this happen?

Could you combine the solution with another idea to produce something new?

* Can the best part be made better?
* Can the worst part be eliminated?
* Can you do this in a bolder or more adventurous way?

Can the solution be made less cumbersome, less involved, less tedious?

8. Follow up and assess your approach.

What do you think of your solution and of your performance? What have you learned? Did the approach work as you expected?

Has the solution worked? If not, how did it fail, and why?

* If the solution failed, did this cause problems elsewhere and if so, what will you do about it?

* If the solution failed, can an emergency plan be patched together until a new solution is ready?

In what ways are you wiser as a result of this failure?

If the solution was a success, could it lead to better things?

* What new opportunities does the solution lead to? How can you exploit these?

* If the solution was a success, does this give you a chance to head off other possible problems?

Will your solution stand the test of time? What happens when you view it in a broader perspective?

Does everyone involved understand the situation?

* What were the best qualities of your appraoch? Efficiency? Speed? Interest? Enjoyment?

* What were the bad qualities of your approach? Misdirection? Cumbersomeness? Disorganization? Lack of inspiration?

Did you try to cut out activities that did not contribute directly to overall objectives? Did you concentrate on activities that did contribute?

* Did you approach the problem in the most effective way? Did you take the best course of action?

How might you have done this faster? How might you have finished this earlier?

Did you go into the problem in sufficient depth?

* Did you dither around? Could your work have been more concentrated?

How can you learn from this situation and so benefit in the future?

Now that the problem is solved, does the world look different to you? How could you benefit from this new view?

* Can you improve the way you tackle problems so that you can devise better solutions faster in the future?

* Can you benefit from others who have experienced similar situations? What did they learn? How can you find out?

Straightforward but Pressured

When you're under pressure, you have more things to keep watch for, and can experience greater worry and distress. In such circumstances, it's easy to think poorly. There's a tendency to be less organized, less careful, less imaginative and to operate generally at a lower level. These tendencies are taken into account in the following strategy, which contains the basic "Straightforward" strategy, along with ways to develop preparedness for crisis and disruption and the possible need to take action before you're ready. The questions are designed to take you quickly to your goal. Then the strategy directs you, if circumstances permit, to an improvement of your solution.

After some section headings, micro-strategy numbers appear in parentheses. The micro-strategies referred to are suggestions for use, as a whole or in part, if you wish to expand the section. Using the micro-strategies in this way will enable you to adjust the emphasis of your strategy somewhat, depending on your circumstances and the size of your problem. For a fast route through the strategy, use only the questions marked with an asterisk.

For protection against frequent interruption, at intervals make a note of your position and ideas so that you won't forget them. The strategies are divided into segments to provide stopping points.

Outline of tasks
1. Prepare for crisis.
2. Set objectives.
3. Seek information.

4. Reassess the immediate situation.
5. Plan.
6. Reassess your progress.
   6-1. Reassess the immediate situation.
   6-2. Reconsider the problem.
   6-3. Check out your solution.
7. Act.
8. Take stock.

1. Prepare for crisis.

Unpredictable things can happen and you should have a contingency plan for dealing with them. Work through these questions as a way of planning your response to emergency.

* What must be rescued or protected to guarantee survival of basic functions and purposes? What are the basic and important areas?
* Can you reduce the range of issues requiring your immediate attention? What is vital to survival?
* Can you tease out, identify, and tackle a central problem, activity, or function, or a group of these? What is the crux of this matter?
* What is the *least* that must be done?
* How will you deal with this emergency and future ones? How will you organize things? What steps will you take?

   What information will you need to remain aware of what is happening?

   How will you decide whether you should act, and what action you might take?

2. Set objectives.

Figure out what you are trying to achieve and the direction you hope to move in.

* What are you trying to do? What issues are you struggling with? What do you hope to achieve?
* Is there anything in your objectives that is ambiguous, conflicting, or inconsistent?

   What would your proposed new situation look like?

   What will be your signs of success? How will you decide when you have resolved things?

* If you can reach only some of your objectives, what will be your priorities?

3. Seek information.
Pin down the issues. Don't set off with only a vague and hasty perception of the problem.
 * What do you already know?
 * What could you quickly find out?
 * What seems to be happening? What difficulties does this cause? What opportunities does this present?
   Where is it all taking place?
   When is it taking place?

   How is it taking place?
 * How long do the events last? How are they timed?
   At what rate are things moving?
 * Why might this be happening?
   Who does this? Who is responsible?

   Who might be causing it?
   What does the overall situation look like?
 * Which areas seem to be the main trouble-spots, or apparent or potential trouble-spots?
 * What are the components and who are the participants of this problem? How many are there?
 * What are the most critical or noteworthy aspects of this problem? Why?
 * How complicated does this problem seem to be? How many components, divisions, or levels does it seem to have?
 * How has the problem developed?
   When did it start?
   How do you know your information is correct and unbiased?
 * Is there anything that you're not sure about or that you don't know?

4. Reassess the immediate situation.
Keep your eyes open. Stay alert. Make sure you get as much warning as possible of impending shifts in the situation.
 * Has the situation changed? Must you take immediate action?

Does the situation look as though it's changing or about to change?

Has the situation already changed in a manner that's hard to recognize? Is it different even though it seems the same?

Has the situation remained fundamentally the same despite apparent changes?

* How might the situation change in a way that would surprise you? What might happen? What would be your weakest spot?

What could you do to be ready for this?

* Do you now have to reorganize, rearrange, or reschedule any part of the current effort? Do you have to change priorities, expand, contract?

5. Plan.

Pull together imaginatively and carefully all the pieces of this puzzle and develop equally imaginative and careful action plans to resolve your difficulties (Micro-Strategy 13).

What is happening in the short term that you will have to deal with?

* What are the things that you know or suspect you must do? Make a list of these details.

* What are these things a part of? Where do they fit? What links one thing to another?

What will happen in the longer term that you will have to deal with?

Can you divide these activities or events into different areas, groups, types, activities, or problems?

* How are these detailed actions related to your larger objectives? Which larger objectives is each of these detailed actions designed to further?

* What are your overall objectives? What are the steps along the way?

What intermediate goals must you reach to achieve these objectives?

* What activities are required for you to achieve your objectives or your intermediate goals?

* Can you break down these objectives and intermediate goals into more detailed activity requirements?

Can you lay out a flowchart, hierarchy, or breakdown of the sub-problems, sub-components, or decisions to be made?

Can you attach to this model the possible choices and outcomes?

What activities are critical to survival? Which activities support your major goals?

* Can you rate the tasks in order of importance? What priority does each one have?

Which parts must interlock?

* Which activities need careful scheduling or timing? What would be the best scheduling and timing of them?

* Can you look into the future and see what might thwart your plans?

* What might you have missed? Is there an area you haven't thought about?
  Can you produce an overall picture of the problem and see clearly how all the parts fit together?
* Can you develop other routes to your overall objectives—intermediate goals, for example—so that when one route is blocked, another might still be open?
  How many alternate routes to your goals can you develop?
* Can you now develop a preferred plan and a couple of backup plans?

6. Reassess your progress.
Don't relax your vigilance. Don't become overconfident. The events around you, your interpretation of the situation, or flaws in the solution you have chosen, could turn the world upside down. Be on your guard.

6-1. REASSESS THE IMMEDIATE SITUATION.
* Has the situation changed? Must you take immediate action?
  Are any new patterns appearing? If so, what do they look like?
  Is there anything going on that may soon involve your situation?
  Do you see any surprises on the way?
* If you can foresee something going wrong, how will you handle it, either to prevent happening or to deal with it afterwards?
* Is anything falling behind? Is anything getting out of step? If so, what will the effect be? What will you do about it?

6-2. RECONSIDER THE PROBLEM.
* What are you trying to do?
  Why do you see this as a problem? What objectives are not being achieved?
* Do you have any facts or information at hand that could show that the situation is not what it seems?
  Is there anything that is so much a part of the accepted way of looking at things that it cannot be considered an issue?
* Do you think you have a firm grasp of what is happening?

* Do you have misgivings about your information? If so, examine the uncertain area carefully. Does your examination lead to different interpretations?

Have your "facts" been confirmed or supported by additional sources or means?

What might you still be unaware of? Is there anything you are unsure of?

* Who could give you another outlook on this situation?

What other things might your interpretation of the situation imply or lead to? Can you find evidence for this? Does considering this question lead to new avenues of inquiry?

How many ways of seeing this problem can you think of?
* Does thinking of other ways to see the problem raise deeper issues than the ones you've been considering?
* Are things really more complicated than this or more simple? Can you see any distinct patterns?
* Are there any odd coincidences?

Is there a core of complexity?
* Which part of your problem is most disturbing and why?

Have you checked up on this area, even though most people may feel sure about it?
* Can you see contradictions or inconsistencies?

Do you have the problem upside down?

6-3. CHECK OUT YOUR SOLUTION.

* Is your proposal doomed from the outset?

Is this solution what you really want? Is it really what is required?

* What are the greatest risks, the greatest challenges? Can these be handled?

* Can you find loose ends? What are you going to do about them?

Is any part of your proposal inconsistent or at odds with any other part?

* Are you seriously considering more than one solution, or have you rushed for the one that seems to solve the most

immediate aspects of the problem, or for the first appealing answer that sprang to mind?

* Did you do your research properly?

Is this solution really as imaginative as you think?

Is this solution really as comprehensive as you think?

Are you resisting the possibility that you will have to throw it all out and start again?

* Are there other ideas about this problem that draw the opposite or different conclusions from your idea?

* Are there other ideas that come close to your idea, or that have been put into action to handle your concerns?

How does your idea measure up to these other ideas? What do you make of the comparison?

How have others gone further than you? Why?

* Will your solution solve the problem, transfer it, or hide it?

* How will you make your solution operate?

Have you worked out in detail the plans and organization of the implementation?

* What actions and stages are required? How will you prevent these from becoming unsynchronized?

If replanning seems necessary at this stage, return to 5 of this strategy.

7. Act.

Should you or have you planned to act now? If so, take action and then use the questions in 8, "Take stock" to consider the results of your action. If you will not be acting right away, you may wish to return to 6, "Reassess," or to 3, "Seek information."

8. Take stock.

Now look at your progress. Can you do even better? Can you remedy any mistakes? What can you learn from your experiences?

* Are you achieving your overall objectives?

* Have your actions had the required effects? If not, why did

they fail? How long did things survive and why?
Does the reason for failure present you with insights or new
   perspectives?
If your actions were a success can you do still better?
* Have your actions or their effects presented any new oppor-
   tunities? If so, what can you do to exploit these?

* Were your actions really effective, or are appearances deceiving you?
Did something just happen or change? If so, will it have an
   effect or not? Where does this event or change fit? What
   could be done about it?
* Must you implement your crisis plan? Do you have a crisis
   plan? If not, use Micro-Strategy 6 to devise one.
* Imagine that the situation, events, or participants are conspiring to surprise you. What would be your weakest spot?
   What might happen?
What could you do to be ready for this?

* What else is going on? Is it significant? Could you connect
   your situation to this other thing going on, either by dis-
   covering subtle links or by making an innovation?
What would happen if the problem situation suddenly dete-
   riorated or if it suddenly improved?
* If you can foresee something going wrong, can you think of
   a way of handling it or preventing it?
* Have you gained new perspectives? Does any new viewpoint
   make a new solution or a new approach seem possible?
Must any new problems be solved?
* If so, how will you organize the solving of them?
* Must you organize, rearrange, or reschedule part of the cur-
   rent effort? Must you change priorities, expand, contract?
* Did you solve this problem in the most effective way? Did
   you take the best course of action?
Did you try to cut out the activities that did not contribute
   directly to overall objectives? Did you concentrate on the
   activities that did?
* Can you improve the way you tackle problems so that you
   can devise better solutions faster in the future?

Complex

In a complex situation, many parts are interlinked, to a greater or lesser degree. Much of the effort required to resolve the situation goes into teasing out these interactions and deciding which are the critical relationships, which the less important ones. Sometimes the interconnections change, thus complicating the situation further. To figure out the interrelationships at one point in time may not be sufficient if the way things fit together keeps changing. You then must look at how and why these changes occur.

This strategy is designed to direct you through the maze of interactions. You begin by taking an apparently central issue and working outward from it. The first goal is to put together a model or picture of the situation and to see if the model can be made to imitate the actual situation. As you work with your problem, focus on the central difficulties, seek out the important interactions, try to find an overall pattern, and persevere until you succeed. You may need to work through this strategy a few times before you're happy with the way you've figured out the problem.

After some section headings, micro-strategy numbers appear in parentheses. The micro-strategies referred to are suggestions for use, as a whole or in part, if you wish to expand the section. Using the micro-strategies in this way will enable you to adjust the emphasis of your strategy somewhat, depending on your circumstances and the size of the problem. For a fast route through the strategy, use only the questions marked with an asterisk.

For protection against frequent interruption, at intervals make a note of your position and ideas so that you won't forget them. The strategies are divided into segments to provide stopping points.

Outline of tasks
1. Set objectives
2. Take a quick look at the situation.
3. Find a focus.
4. Break out the sub-problems.
5. Stay organized.
    5-1. Remain watchful.
6. Pick out a problem to focus on.
7. Examine interactions.
    7-1. Interactions among sub-problems.
    7-2. Interactions with neighboring systems.
8. Make a model of the situation as you now perceive it.
9. Look for an overall pattern.
10. Solve each sub-problem.
11. Stay organized.
12. Review solutions to sub-problems.
    12-1. Explore sub-problem solutions for conflict and coverage.
    12-2. Develop a coordinated solution.
    12-3. Prepare implementation plans.
13. Test your solutions on your model.
    13-1. Review interactions in the context of the proposed solutions.
14. Assess and improve your solution.
15. Follow up and assess your approach.

1. Set objectives.
Even if goals are clear, a complex situation can be hectic. If you don't clarify what you are trying to achieve, and keep that picture in mind, your disorientation will defeat you (Micro-Strategy 2).
* What are you trying to do? What issues are you struggling with? What do you hope to achieve?
  What are your short-terms goals?
  What are your long-term goals?

Are your goals realistic? For yourself? For other participants?
* What do you want the proposed new situation to look like?

* Are your objectives in any way inconsistent or at odds with each other?
* What will by your signs of success? How will you decide when you have resolved things?
  What measure of success will you be satisfied with?
* If you can achieve only some of your objectives, what are your priorities?

2. Take a quick look at the situation.
Before you become involved in the intricacies of interlocking details, make a first exploration by trying to learn the geography

HOOT SAYS:

FOR A COMPLEX PROBLEM

1. BREAK IT DOWN INTO SMALLER PIECES IN SOME WAY.
2. LOOK AT WHAT THE FIRST PIECE IS ALL ABOUT.
3. LOOK AT WHAT THE SECOND PIECE IS ALL ABOUT CONTINUE THIS WITH ALL REMAINING PIECES.
4. LOOK AT HOW ALL THE PIECES FIT TOGETHER AND INFLUENCE EACH OTHER.
5. IN THE LIGHT OF STEP 4 — THE OVERALL PICTURE — REVIEW ANY PUZZLING PIECES OR MISFITS.
6. IN THE LIGHT OF STEP 5 — THE DETAILS — REVIEW ANY PUZZLING CONNECTIONS IN THE OVERALL PICTURE.

of the overall situation.
* What do you already know about this situation?
* What could you quickly find out?
  What seem to be the objectives of this operation, framework, structure, or system?
* What is this problem's place in the general scheme of things?
* What are the components and who are the participants of this problem? How many are there?
  How does each part interact with the others?
  What can be inferred from these interactions? What is implied? Where do these things lead?

* Can you identify and describe all the information pathways?
* Can you identify and describe time scales, rhythms, or flows in activities or in the way this situation changes shape?
* What decision processes are involved? What controls, influences, or organization?
* What uncertainties, unpredictabilities, or instabilities are there?

* Can you see contradictions or inconsistencies?
* Is there a center of organization or control? Is there a central trouble spot or weak point?
* Does your response to these questions raise deeper issues?
  What hidden or unstated goals or directions might there be?
* What might be some of the long-term effects, influences, and interactions?
  Have you considered what might be happening outside the immediate problem area? What other involvements might there be?
* Can you see distinct patterns?
  Can you think of a simple explanation of this problem?
  Are things really more complicated than this? Or simpler?
* Have you missed anything?
* Is there a technique, procedure, theory, principle, or concept already developed and available that would enable you to deal with the problem speedily and effectively?
* Is there a skill that you have or that someone else you can call upon has that would enable you to deal with this problem speedily and effectively?

3. Find a focus.
You cannot start everywhere at once, yet you must start some-where. The focus you select at the beginning can be discarded, if necessary, when you achieve new, clearer perceptions. So, begin with a sense of direction.

* Can you reduce the range of issues requiring your immediate attention? What seems to be the central concern?

    What gives meaning to your life or your operation? What do you care deeply about? Is there a higher objective or prin-ciple that can guide you? Can you use this as a point to focus on?

* Can you identify the things that you cannot do anything about immediately, the things that are not under your con-trol or influence? If so, can you leave these areas alone for now? (Not for ever!)

    Is there a common thread running through all your problems, that is, are all or many of your difficulties related in some way?

    Can you tease out, identify, and describe this central prob-lem, or group of problems?

* How can you simplify the problem without oversimplifying it?

* What seem to be the most central and critical aspects of this problem? Why?

4. Break out the sub-problems.
First, select the best way to subdivide the overall situation. Identify the pieces.

* How complicated does this problem seem to be? How many components, divisions, or levels does it seem to have? De-tail these.

    Which interrelationships are close and strong? Which are loose and weak?

    Which interrelationships are unchanging? Which ones change, fluctuate, become modified, or could do these things?

    Which interrelationships seem clear and which are hard to pin down?

* Can you arrange the components and interrelationships in or-der of importance? Which part affects the greatest number

of other parts? Which part has the strongest effects or influence?

* What is connected to what? Can you draw a map, diagram, flowchart, or picture of the pieces? Can you see how each one is, or might be, connected to the others? Are there any missing connections?
Are you seeing relationships or interactions correctly?
Is this the best way of viewing these pieces and relationships?
How else could it be done?
Does everything have to be dealt with at this point?

Can you split up the problem situation into distinct categories, types, or areas of difficulty? Detail these.
* Can you break the problem situation into sub-problems or smaller parts that can safely be dealt with separately? Detail these sub-problems.
* When the problem is broken up into pieces, what must be kept in mind, what conditions must be set up, or what objectives must be achieved so that the sub-problems can be dealt with individually and later pulled together for an integrated solution?

5. Stay organized.

As you become acquainted with the situation, it may overwhelm and disorient you. This section is a reminder to keep your directions clear.
* Where are you trying to go?
* What will you do next? Why? Where does this action fit in the overall plan and/or in the sub-problem?
* Are you changing course or tactics with insufficient justification, or too frequently?
* Are you moving inflexibly, following a fixed pattern?
* Are you noting possible new directions, dangers, concerns, or ideas?

5-1. REMAIN WATCHFUL.

Think about the following questions in two ways: first, in the sense of watching what is going on around you; second, in the sense of watching and coordinating your own efforts.

Have you a plan for staying organized through major disruption, whether this interruption be voluntary or involuntary? How will you keep track of where you were and what you were thinking when the interruption occurred?

* What information do you need in order to remain aware of what is happening?

How will you be able to see, predict, or find out about what might happen next?

How will you decide what your information or news is indicating?

* How will you decide whether you should act, and what action you should take?

Is this situation moving on a collision course with anything else? How can this be avoided?

6. Pick out a problem to focus on.
Now that you have felt your way toward what you believe to be the core of the matter, maximize your effectiveness by concentrating all your energy on one focal point at a time. Then organize and schedule these pieces of the situation.

Can you pull out, identify, and tackle a central problem, or group of problems?

* Which areas look as though they'll need the most time, the most energy?

* Can you cover all the parts? If not, which ones should you concentrate on?

* Which activities need careful scheduling or timing? What would be the best scheduling and timing of them?

Which activities can be fitted in with the least difficulty?

Which activities will have the most uncertain, unpredictable, or unstable consequences?

What are the important activities?

Have you identified anything that might become vital if things change? Are your plans flexible?

* Which activities will have the greatest impact if they succeed? If they fail? If they are delayed, disorganized, rearranged?

How long will each action take? If you don't know, will your uncertainty affect the way things fit together? What precautions must you take?

Have you thought out what you will do if you miss one of your targets?

* Which parts must be kept in harmony with each other?
* Which parts or people could give each other support? How can this mutual benefit be arranged?

Which parts might undermine each other? Can this wastefulness be avoided?

What will you do to make sure the separate parts of the project interlink smoothly?

* How should action be organized? What timing is necessary?
* How must the tasks be arranged and sequenced for best effect? Can this be done?
* How might you order the sub-problems to maximize the ben-

efits that a simultaneous attack on all or some of them
would bring to the sub-problems and to the problem as a
whole?

* Should a group of people do this?
  Who could be on the team?
  How will the team operate? How will it be put together?
  What objectives, responsibilities, scope, privileges, and au-
  thority will each team member have?

  How far will this project reach? What will be its boundaries?
  When will you carry it out?
  How will you carry it out?
* What target dates, amounts, or positions are there?
* How will you assess your progress?
* What output will be produced?
  How long will it take?

7. Examine interactions.

Look at the interactions between sub-problems, between sub-
problems and the overall situation, and between the overall situation and surrounding events. In a complex problem, the interactions between parts is important enough to be viewed as a
sub-problem in its own right. This investigation of interactions
should be done separately from your other procedures so that it
doesn't disturb your concentration on each sub-problem. The
questions in this section should help you to look at the parts
and see how they're tied together. Give each phase your undi-
vided attention, or you'll end up going around in circles, or
feeling paralyzed by the complexity of the situation.

7-1. INTERACTIONS AMONG SUB-PROBLEMS.

You may wish also to use these questions in 7-2, when you're
thinking about larger problem interactions.
* What relationship does each part have with each other part?
  What information passes back and forth? What activity patterns are there?
* What are the most important sub-problems, parts, relationships, outcomes?

* Are there other things connected to each sub-problem, either directly or indirectly?

What is the nature or manner of these connections?

How closely connected to each sub-problem are these other sub-problems, events, principles, functions, concepts?

* How strong are the associations or interactions?

Why are things related to each other in the ways that they are?

* How did the present relationships or arrangements of events develop?

Do all these parts or sub-problems fit together in a coherent pattern? Do they all interact smoothly? Are there any misfits?

Is there a lasting pattern? Does any relationship, value, structural arrangement, function, or process endure?

* Do things always interact in the same way, or do their interactions change, oscillate, or fluctuate?

Are things connected permanently and stably? Or intermittently, haphazardly, arbitrarily, or irregularly?

* How do quantities, values, arrangements, or characteristics change? What specific value or values do they assume?

* Is there a central focus of complexity?

* Is the complexity in this situation mainly of one type? For example, does complexity result mainly from the numbers of parts that are interacting, changes of those parts that are interconnected, changes of how parts are connected, or changes of rates of interaction?

7-2. INTERACTIONS WITH NEIGHBORING SYSTEMS.

Go through these questions once to examine interactions of each sub-problem with the overall situation, and once to examine interactions of the overall situation with its context.

What is this problem's place in the general scheme of things?

Do other systems, structures, functions, or frameworks directly influence this situation? Are any of them influenced by it?

Do other systems, structures, functions, or frameworks indirectly influence or interact with this situation?

* Which parts, pieces, systems, persons, or events control, influence, or motivate others?

* How are related or interacting situations developing? What is happening in them?
* What connections, interactions, traffic flow, or interchange is there between this situation and its surroundings? Can these things be changed?

  Why is the framework, institution, culture, or system that contains this problem set up the way it is? What effects does this structure have on the problem? Can this structure and its relationships be changed? Might they change anyway? What would happen if they did?

  If you rearranged the surroundings of your problem, would the problem disappear?
* What assumptions are you making about the context in which this situation is taking place? Are they valid?
* What structures, processes, and people hold this situation together?
* Does the situation that contains the problem lack harmony? Are things out of step, in conflict, at odds with each other, out of balance?
* If there is a lack of harmony, is it reasonable? Could the condition be changed? If so, in how many ways? If not, why not?

  Is this a real or sufficient reason?

8. Make a model of the situation as you now perceive it.

By constructing a detailed model, picture, flowchart, or structure of some kind, you can make plain the workings of your situation in a manner that should make it easier to struggle with.

  Do you have a clear picture of what you are trying to achieve? What specific state of affairs are you trying to achieve?
* Can you identify and describe *all* the components and participants in this situation?

  Can you identify and describe *all* the information pathways?
* Can you identify and describe *all* the interactions between the various parts, showing what happens if and when they interact?

  Can you identify and describe time scales, rhythms, or flows in activities, or in the way this situation changes shape?

* Can you assess the importance or priority of each part? Which part affects the greatest number of other parts? Which part has the strongest effects or influence?

  What decision processes, controls, or influences are involved?
  What uncertainties, unpredictabilities or instabilities are there?
* How do the pieces and activities fit together and harmonize, or fail to, in an overall movement, rhythm, or operation?
* How can each part, pathway, function, flow, or rhythm be represented? By a chart, graph, flowchart, formula, drawing, scale model, working model, game, play?
  Can you build a working model that is a mathematical, physical or philosophical structure?
  Which kind of modeling seems most appropriate to the situ-

ation? Which kind handles the situation's complexity or abstraction properly?

* Can you lay out a hierarchy, flowchart, picture, or breakdown of possible choices and outcomes?
* How can actual processes, functions, time scales, and activities be represented in the model?
  How can the structure and workings of the actual situation or of the new proposal be imitated?
  How much of your situation and its processes can your model represent?
* Can you operate your model in different ways, to gain a clear picture of how things might be operating in actuality?
  Does your model clarify fundamental relationships and processes? Are any relationships or processes still vague and fuzzy?

* If there is any uncertainty, chance, unpredictability, or instability in part of the situation, is the condition properly represented or even recognized? Can you imitate or simulate the condition by using dice, cards, or random-number tables?
* How far must you test your model before you can accept it as a picture of the real situation? Be ingenious.
* When you operate the model, simulating the flows, changes, rhythms, and uncertainties of life, does your model respond properly? That is, does it give results comparable to the real actions, and does it predict and act in a plausible, realistic manner?
  How closely can your model represent life without being too cumbersome or complicated to operate quickly and simply?
  If you cannot make your model detailed or complex enough to represent life, are you trying to model the wrong processes or using the wrong kind of modeling?
  Can the model easily reflect the kinds of changes that take place in actuality?

9. Look for an overall pattern.
Be aware at all times of the value of searching for patterns. Try

to keep a map laid out before you, to avoid feeling as though you're stumbling through a maze. Seek patterns and coherence continuously. Finding an appealing pattern may alter your view of how the problem situation can be broken down, and may thus prompt you to make a different arrangement of sub-problems (Micro-Strategy 12).

  Could you use a broader perspective? Could this problem be seen as part of a larger system? Is there a higher level of interpretation, a more inclusive process for looking at the problem?

* Can you see an overall pattern, a structure, a key to reducing the complexity of the situation?

  Can you alter the context in which this situation is taking place? That is, can you restructure the whole pattern so that the problem is eliminated, bypassed, or rendered irrelevant?

* Is there another way to look at this situation that might throw a different light on it? That is, could the situation be seen as part of a different issue? Could it be an opportunity in disguise, a chance to get something different straightened out? Try hard to look at the problem in a different way.

* What might happen next? In the near future? In the long term?

* Might the future of this situation differ considerably from the past?

  How might future developments affect this situation?

  What else might you be able to construct from this situation?

* Can you change the angle that you're taking on this problem? What is your present angle? Emotional, geographical, rational, personal, chronological, organizational, political, ethical?

  Have you experienced anything similar to this?

* Look out the window. Let the first thing you see set your thoughts about the problem on a new path.

* Are there any strange coincidences?

* How can you modify the scope or boundaries of the problem? How can you expand it or contract it? Could this help to provide a fresh perspective?

What indirect or unusual approach can you take with this difficulty? What unexpected angles could you try?
* What does the problem look like from the other end? Can you turn the situation upside down?

10. Solve each sub-problem.

Now that you've broken out the sub-problems, you should be facing a group of comparatively small problems. If so, then work on each problem using Strategy 1, "Straightforward." If a sub-problem does not fit in this "Straightforward" category, then turn to Section 6, "What Kind of Situation Are You in?" and use the procedures there to select a more appropriate strategy for the sub-problem. After you have followed that strategy, proceed with 11, "Stay organized," in this strategy.

11. Stay organized.

Depending on the complexity of your situation, you should from time to time review what you've been doing and where you are going so that your problem-solving behavior remains coherent.
* Where are you trying to go?
  What are the broad outlines of your approach? Have these been changing?
  What are the main pieces of your plan and where do they fit?
* What are you going to do next? Why? Where does this action fit in the overall plan and/or in the sub-problem?
  Are any parts overlapping or interwoven? What are you doing to keep these relationships straight?
  Are you looking at things at different levels, without confusing these different levels?
* Are you changing course or tactics with insufficient justification or too frequently?
* Are you moving inflexibly, following a fixed pattern?
  What tasks are outstanding? What may you have missed?

* Are you keeping a note of possible new directions, dangers, concerns, or ideas?
* Have you adhered to your plan for staying organized through major disruption? How will you keep track of where you were and what you were thinking if disruption occurs?

Could you work on this problem more effectively, more competently? Could you take more telling action?

Is anything slipping? Organization, motivation, timing, imagination, judgment, critical review?

* Is your effort moving on a collision course with anything else?

Is there a central idea or unifying theme that allows you to keep track of what you are trying to do?

Should you reorganize your efforts for better effect?

Are you keeping in mind your reason for solving this problem, or are you being diverted from the main issues?

12. Review solutions to sub-problems.

By now you no doubt have some solutions to your sub-problems. When you consider all these solutions in concert, you may encounter conflict between some, as well as areas that have not been covered. These difficulties must be reviewed, and all the sub-problem solutions brought together and arranged to produce a coherent solution. This may mean re-solving some sub-problems if they cannot be made to harmonize with the whole picture. Alternatively, this maladjustment of the sub-problem solutions may cause you to consider whether you have misunderstood the overall situation (Micro-Strategy 13).

12-1. EXPLORE SUB-PROBLEM SOLUTIONS FOR CONFLICT AND COVERAGE.

* What may you have missed?
* Are you achieving your overall objectives?

What might there be that you don't know? What are you unsure of?

Does your problem strategy still suit the problem situation?

* Will this solution have effects anywhere else?

Have you considered what, if any, trade-offs must be made for each alternative?

* How does everything interact? How is everything tied together? Are there any missing connections?

How does each part relate to, interact with, or connect with each other part?

* What else is interwoven in these relationships? Are there any direct influences?

* What is the nature or manner of these interconnections?
  What can be inferred from these interconnections? What is
  implied by them? What do they lead to?
* What is your assessment of the benefit, potential, priority,
  cost, and impact of each major part and interaction?

12-2. DEVELOP A COORDINATED SOLUTION.
* What is required here? What needs must be satisfied? What
  conditions met? What must be taken care of?
  Where are the relevant ideas and information that you have
  so far? Can you pull them all together?
  Out of this material can you extract what seem to be the cen-
  tral issues?
* Can you clarify things by arranging the ideas or information
  around these central issues?
* What are the important parts, relationships, or outcomes?
  What are the priorities? What is the crux of the matter?
  Which leads look as though they'll guide you in the most
  fruitful direction? Where are the best ideas, explanations or
  contributions for your solution likely to be found?

* How do you think all this fits together? Have you a first guess
  or a hunch to test out?
  Can you think of a metaphor or analogy that could start you
  pulling things together?
  Can you see a simple form in this, some underlying process?
* Is there a pattern you can pick out or invent to explain this?
* Which parts must be kept in harmony with each other?
  How many separate parts, sub-sections, and connections
  should the solution have?
  How many levels of organization should the solution have?
  That is, should it take the form of a pyramid, or a hierarchy
  of linked sub-systems in which some sub-systems direct
  others?

  Which parts could give each other support? Can this mutual
  benefit be arranged?
  Which parts might undermine each other? Can this wastefulness be avoided?

* Consider whether you have covered the following elements of the problem:

—the way the parts will fit together, interlock, or interact. Do these parts form a coherent structure, that is, do their interactions, functions, processes, and patterns make sense?

—the total structure. Is it a good pattern? Is it harmonious? What coordinates the structure? What processes hold it together?

—information flows or channels. Communications? Messages? Is information transmitted quickly, clearly, to the right places, and without redundancy?

—decisions, control, organization. How will the parts stay together? How will the situation keep going?

—uncertainty, unpredictability. Have you planned for trouble?

—growth, change, evolution. How will the situation develop or be developed? What are you going to do to promote development?

* In what areas should you clarify, elaborate, develop further ideas? What fuzzy areas are left?

What must you still decide about?

* Can you list the outstanding tasks in priority sequence? Will anyone resent or resist this solution? Why?

* Can you think of a better idea to tie all this together? Can you improve your original concept?

How might you achieve deeper insights?

Could you take a broader look at all this?

Could your resolution be more extensive?

12-3. PREPARE IMPLEMENTATION PLANS (MICRO-STRATEGY 19).

* What are your targets? How much time do you need? Have you set deadlines? What are your priorities?

* Which areas need the most attention? Which might give the most difficulty?

* Which activities need careful scheduling or timing? What would be the best scheduling and timing of them?

* Which parts will have the greatest impact if they succeed? If

they fail? If they are delayed, disorganized, rearranged?
How do you plan to make your solution operate?
* Should you give this proposal a trial run before installing a
full-scale solution?
Can you put your new idea in action alongside the old situation to compare the two, to test the new idea, or to phase
the new idea in gradually?

What actions and stages are required? How will you prevent
these from becoming unsynchronized?
What will you do to make sure the separate parts of the proj-
ect interlink smoothly?
* Have you a plan for assessing the solution's success?
Does everyone affected understand and accept the changes
that might occur?
How will you keep track of progress?
* How will you keep an eye open for the unanticipated? What
will you do?
* If you can foresee something going wrong, do you have a way
of handling it or preventing it?

13. Test your solutions on your model.
Now that you think you have solved the component problems,
put everything together and see how the situation looks when
you test it on your model. Use 8 in this strategy to make models
of your solutions, or to make the solutions fit a model you already have. The following questions might also be useful in
testing your solutions.
For each point at which a decision is to be made, what are
the benefits, risks, and uncertainties involved?
How might you improve the model? Could the actual situation be improved in the same way?
Have you unintentionally missed any aspect of the problem?
What resources are used, what costs incurred, or what danger
courted by each solution?
What is the benefit, potential, priority, cost, and impact of
each part of the model and each interaction between parts?

13-1. REVIEW INTERACTIONS IN THE CONTEXT OF PROPOSED SOLUTIONS.

Repeat all of 7 in this strategy to see how well your modeled solutions are doing.

14. Assess and improve your solution.

Because this problem is complex, because you don't want to have to rework it all later, and because the solution's impact will be large, you must now seek hidden flaws and try to improve the solution. Questions that seem to be duplicating previous ones are included to ensure that you take a second look at areas that may have changed as the jigsaw puzzle was put together.

Is this solution what you really want? Is it really what is needed?

* Does it contain a coherent whole, or pattern, or explanation? Does it hang together properly?

* Can you find loose ends? What are you going to do about them?

Could you take a wider outlook? Are you looking at the situation from too narrow a perspective?

* Are things really more complicated than this, or simpler?

* Will the solution have by-products, side effects or aftereffects? What will they be? How will you handle them?

* Are you seriously considering more than one solution, or have you rushed for the one that seems to solve the most immediate aspects of the problem, or for the first appealing answer that sprang to mind?

Is anything within this solution at odds with itself? Do any of the solution's objectives or procedures conflict with each other?

Are you slipping into self-justification efforts, avoidance, or rationalization in what you are doing?

Will the solution have effects elsewhere?

* Is this solution moving on a collision course with anything else?

How might the solution be affected by something connected to it?

* Have you considered what, if any, trade-offs may have to be made for each alternative? Have you balanced the interests in the best way?
* What resources are used, what costs incurred, or what danger courted by each alternative?

  Will this idea continue to work in the future?

  Can you foresee any disasters for your solution? How would you avoid these?

  If future events were to take a turn for the better, would you be able to take full advantage of this?
* What would happen if the problem situation suddenly deteriorated, or if it suddenly improved?
* What are the areas of accelerating growth of the situation, that is, where are important changes taking place? How many are there, and what effects might they have? Which ones are interwoven or interdependent? How vigorous is their growth? Which ones will have the greatest impact on your solution? How might your solution be forced to take them into account?
* Can you think of a variety of ways in which the future might unfold? Can your solution handle these possibilities?

* Can you think of ways in which your solution might make things worse?

  Is the solution flexible? Does it permit smooth handling of changing internal and external circumstances?

  Does the solution make things simpler? Does it make things clearer?

  If it is not possible to think of a better plan or solution, and there are still some uncertain areas, can you develop ideas to deal with the risks?

  When challenged by difficulty or crisis, will this plan, system, or solution maintain its organization and its responsiveness, or will it become disorganized and ineffective?
* How long will it take for crisis or potential disaster to be recognized as such?

  How quickly will you be able to respond to a crisis?
* Will the objectives or functions of your plan or solution survive a crisis or disaster even if this requires their taking on

a new expression or form?
* Is this a stopgap solution, or is it firmly grounded in an over-all strategy?
* Does your proposal use up resources that would be better used elsewhere?
* Does your proposal limit anyone's growth or fulfillment?
If your solution involves people, does it do so in such a way that their functioning or rewards will be less than they might be?
Will anyone suffer as a result of this situation?
* Can you find a way to make this solution more effective? More powerful? More significant?
* Can you find a way to make this solution simpler? Is there a simpler answer than this?
Can you find a way to make the solution work more quickly?
Can you find a way to make the solution more flexible?
* Is there a way to make the solution require less energy, attention, or maintenance?
* Is there a way to make the solution do more with the same input?
Can this solution have more widespread or comprehensive benefits? What would be required to make this possible?
Could you combine the solution with another idea to make something new?
* Can the best part be made better?
* Can the worst part be eliminated?
Can the solution be made less cumbersome, less involved, less tedious?
* Can you deal with this problem in a bolder, more adventurous way?

15. Follow up and assess your approach.

In checking out your solution, you should look both at the individual sub-problem solutions and at the overall solution. Use the following questions to examine, one by one, each facet of your problem's resolution.

Has the solution worked? If not, how did it fail and what was the cause?
* If the solution failed, did this cause problems elsewhere and,

if so, what will you do about it?
* If the solution failed, can an emergency plan be patched together until a new solution is ready?

In what ways are you wiser as a result of this failure?

If the solution was a success, can this lead to still better things?
* What new opportunities does the solution lead to? How can you exploit these?

* If the solution was a success, does this give you a chance to head off other possible problems?

Will your solution stand the test of time? How does it look if you view it in a broader perspective?

Does everyone involved fully understand the situation?
* What were the best points about your approach? Efficiency? Speed? Interest? Enjoyment?
* What were the bad points about your approach? Misdirection? Cumbersomeness? Disorganization? Lack of inspiration?

Did you try to cut out activities that did not contribute directly to overall objectives? Did you concentrate on activities that did?
* Did you approach the problem in the most effective way? Did you take the best course of action?

How might you have solved the problem faster? How might you have finished this earlier?

Did you go into the problem in sufficient depth?
* Did you dither around? Could your work have been more concentrated?

How can you learn from this situation and benefit from it in the future?

Now that you've solved your problem, does the world look different to you? How could you benefit from this new view?
* Can you improve the way you tackle problems so that you can devise better solutions faster in the future?
* Can you benefit from others who have experienced similar situations? What did they learn? How can you find out?

HOOT SAYS:

FOR AN UNPREDICTABLE SITUATION OR ONE
WITH MANY UNCERTAINTIES

1. SELECT THE BEST COURSE OF ACTION YOU
   CAN DESPITE THE UNCERTAINTY AND EVEN
   THOUGH YOU MAY NOT FIND IT EASY TO
   JUSTIFY.
2. KEEP TRYING TO PIN DOWN THE
   UNCERTAINTIES AND RISKS.
3. REVIEW YOUR PLAN AND OPERATION
   FREQUENTLY.
4. CULTIVATE OASES OF CALM TO RETREAT
   TO OCCASIONALLY SINCE LIFE IS GOING
   TO BE MUCH MORE OF A STRAIN THAN
   USUAL.

Unpredictable

Unpredictable situations put great pressure on your ability to remain calm and unflustered. The possibility of circumstances changing in an unexpected way without warning makes it difficult to keep your aim on your goals. In such situations, two tasks must be performed in parallel. You must try to figure out the source of the unpredictability. When you know why events bounce around in this uncertain way, you will be in a better position to take control of events and keep them from controlling you. You must also make a set of emergency plans to minimize the disruptions that the unpredictable situation creates. As you work on the problems, you should try to improve these plans. The questions in this strategy switch back and forth from the topics of pattern seeking and unpredictability hunting to the preparation and improvement of your contingency plans. By the end of the strategy you should have your situation pinned down sufficiently to pick out a more structured strategy or micro-strategy that will help you finally solve the problem, if you haven't already done so.

After some section headings, micro-strategy numbers appear in parentheses. The micro-strategies referred to are suggestions for use, as a whole or in part, if you wish to expand the section. Using the micro-strategies in this way will enable you to adjust the emphasis of your strategy somewhat, depending on your circumstances and the size of the problem. For a fast route through the strategy, use only the questions marked with an asterisk.

For protection against frequent interruption, at intervals make a note of your position and ideas so that you won't forget them.

The strategies are divided into segments to provide stopping points.

Outline of tasks
1. Make a crisis plan.
    1-1. What must you defend or rescue?
    1-2. How might this be done?
2. Figure out where you want to go.
3. Diagnose the problem more clearly.
4. Reassess the immediate situation.
5. Take a more thorough look around.
6. Build better crisis and contingency plans.
    6-1. Devolop ideas.
    6-2. Construct plans out of your ideas.
    6-3. Prepare implementation plans.
7. Assess and improve your plans.
8. Reassess the immediate situation.
9. Take a wider look at the total situation.
    9-1. How does all this hang together?
    9-2. What is all this about?
10. Return to the approach-choosing procedure.

1. Make a crisis plan.
Something unpredictable is going to happen, or you are already in an unpredictable situation. How can you guarantee the survival of the things you value? Work through this section and prepare something, even if it's only a way of approaching the situation, in case the unpredictable event turns out to be disastrous. Have a backup plan for sudden emergency.

1-1. WHAT MUST YOU DEFEND OR RESCUE?
Make sure that basic functions and purposes survive.

FIRST LOOK.
 * What activities, functions, people, items, or relationships must you preserve or rescue?
 * What is required to do this?
 * How might you accomplish this?

KEEP YOUR EYES OPEN.

To become more flexible and adaptable in your responses, you need information that can help you predict what will happen next. Be watchful.

* What information do you need to remain aware of what is happening?

    How will you be able to see, predict, or find out about what might happen next?

    How will you decide what your information or news indicates?

* How will you decide whether you should act, and what action you might take?

SECOND LOOK.

* What gives meaning to your life or operation? What do you care deeply about? Is there a higher objective or principle that could guide you? Can you use it as a point to focus on?
* Can you reduce the range of issues requiring your immediate attention? What is vital to survival?
* Can you tease out, identify, and tackle a central need, activity, or function, or group of these? What is the crux of the matter?
* What are the fundamentally important areas?
* What is the most that *can* be done?
* What is the least that *must* be done?

1-2. HOW MIGHT THIS BE DONE?

Get organized—and fast.

* Is there a technique, procedure, theory, principle, or concept already developed and available that would allow you to deal with this problem speedily and effectively?
* Is there a skill that you have, or that someone else you could call upon has, that would enable you to deal with this problem speedily and effectively?

    How will you cope with this emergency and any future ones? How will you organize things? What steps will you take?

* How should your action be organized? What timing is necessary?

    Which parts will have the greatest impact if they succeed? If

they fail? If they are delayed, disorganized, rearranged?
* Have you covered the areas that might become vital if things change? Are your plans flexible?
* How can you move fast on this?
   What target dates, amounts, or positions are there?

2. Figure out where you want to go.

Although the world may be running every which way, you presumably have goals of your own. Make sure these goals are clear so that as you begin to control the situation you can turn things more to your advantage (Micro-Strategy 2).
* What are you trying to do? What issues are you struggling with? What do you hope to achieve?
   What would your proposed new situation look like?
* Do you have alternative paths of action? If one way is blocked, would another be satisfactory?
* What will be the key signs of success? Which signs will be less important?
   What are your short-term goals?
   What are your long-term goals?

3. Diagnose the problem more clearly.

Now take a good look at the situation and see if you can grasp more firmly what is going on, and why, and what will happen next (Micro-Strategy 4).
* What does the overall situation look like?
* Why do you see this situation as a problem? What objectives are not being achieved?
* What do you already know?
* What could you quickly find out?
   What are the components and who are the participants of this problem? How many are there?
* What are the most critical or noteworthy aspects of this problem? Why?
* How complicated does this problem seem to be? How many components, divisions, or levels does it seem to have?
   How has this problem developed?
   When did the problem start?

How unpredictable is the situation? Is it completely uncertain, uncertain only within particular areas, or does it have some degree of probability?

In which areas is the most uncertainty?

* Is the unpredictability or uncertainty only at some levels, locations, or times; or involving only some events; or within only some ranges?

How do quantities, values, arrangements, or characteristics change? What values or range of values do they assume?

* Do things always interact in the same way, or do their interactions change, oscillate, or fluctuate?

* Are the parts of the situation connected permanently and stably? Or intermittently, haphazardly, arbitrarily, or irregularly?

Is there a lasting pattern in the situation? Does any relationship, value, structural arrangement or function, or process endure?

* What hidden or unstated goals or directions might there be?

Can you think of a variety of ways in which the future might unfold?

4. Reassess the immediate situation.

Keep your eyes open. Stay alert. Make sure you get as much warning as possible of impending shifts in the situation. If you take crisis action while using this section, or afterward, you may wish, before going on to the approach-choosing procedure in Section 6 or returning to the beginning of this strategy, to follow up your crisis action with a look at Micro-Strategy 24, "Taking stock," which should help you to assess the new situation.

* Has the situation changed? Must you implement your crisis plan?

Does the situation look as though it is changing or about to change?

Has the situation already changed in a manner that's hard to recognize? Is it different even though it seems the same?

Has the situation remained fundamentally the same despite apparent changes?

* In what way that would surprise you can you imagine the situation changing? What would be your weakest spot? What might happen?
  What could you do to be ready for this?
* Must you now reorganize, rearrange, or reschedule any part of the current effort? Must you change priorities, expand, or contract?

5. Take a more thorough look around.
As we have noted, in this strategy, you are alternating between preparing more carefully for crisis, emergency, or sudden change, and trying to determine the roots of the unpredictability in your situation. Here, the activity is seeking out and examining the unpredictability.

* How can you find out about the unpredictability, threat or competition? Is there someone you can talk to about it? Where can you look for information? What can you read, remember, see?
  Can you find the source of the unpredictability, threat, or competition?
* From where and from how many sources is the unpredictability coming?
  Where else might the unpredictability come from in the future?
  Can you isolate the unpredictable part of the situation and stay clear of it, or minimize its impact?
* Who or what is, or might be, causing the unpredictability? Now? In the future?

* What significant new directions could the situation take that would alter the kinds of, and sources of, unpredictability? Where are the areas of accelerating growth?
  Where is the power to change things (other than in yourself) located? What is the source of power doing?
* What else is going on? Is it significant? Could you connect your problem with this other thing going on, either by discovering subtle links or by making an innovation?
* If you can foresee something going wrong, do you have some way of handling it?

* What would happen if the problem situation suddenly deteriorated, or if it suddenly improved?

Does it look as though the future of this situation will differ considerably from the past?

* Can you detect patterns in growth, change, decay, or evolution within this situation?

* Has this problem had serious effects in other areas? What are these effects? What action has been taken in response?

Does looking at the past shed any light on potential problems or developments?

Do some parts of the problem that may not actually be difficulties look like difficulties, or vice versa?

Are you considering which ideas your information supports, and which ones it does *not* support?

* Are you certain that *this* is the real problem? Are you sure that the problem is what it *seems* to be?

* Have you considered what might be happening outside the immediate problem area?

How do you know your information is correct and unbiased?

Is there anything that you're not sure about or that you don't know?

Who could give you another outlook on this situation?

* Can you see any distinct patterns?

Are there any strange coincidences?

Can you find any little things that are out of joint with the rest of the situation, or some small inconsistency where things are otherwise harmonious? What does this mean? Does this flaw affect your picture of the situation?

* Might there be another explanation of this situation?

6. Build better crisis and contingency plans.

The more you comprehend of the situation, the less you'll have to operate on an emergency basis. You'll be more confident as you move into the planning, or contingency planning, phase.

6-1. DEVELOP IDEAS (MICRO-STRATEGIES 9 AND 10).

* Is there another way you could look at this situation that might throw a different light on it? That is, could the situation be seen as part of a different issue? Could the situation be seen as an opportunity in disguise, as a chance to get something different straightened out? Try hard to look at the situation in different ways.

What might a blacksmith, a doctor, or a sailor have to say about this problem?

* What is the most prominent, intriguing, fruitful, or useful aspect of all this? Can you use that aspect to find a new angle?

* Can you change the way you are approaching the problem? For example, if you are faced with traffic problems, would it help to think of designing a new kind of car or a new type of motive power or drive system? Would it help to think about new types of transportation or city design? Can you take both a broader and a more detailed view?

How can you modify the scope or the boundaries of this problem? Can you expand it or contract it? How might this help?

* What indirect or unusual approach could you take with this difficulty? What unexpected angles could you try?
* What does the problem look like from the other end? Can you turn the situation upside down?
* Can you see this problem in a humorous light? Could a more relaxed view of the situation lead to a new perspective on it?

6-2. CONSTRUCT PLANS OUT OF YOUR IDEAS (MICRO-STRATEGIES 11, 8, 14, AND 26).

* What are your targets? How much time do you need? Have you set deadlines? What are your priorities?
* What will be the components and who will be the participants of your new situation? Have you specified these?
* What seem to be the chief points to decide about or wrestle with? What areas are there?
  Can they all be handled? If not, which should be the ones to concentrate on?
* Can you produce a flowchart or decision tree, or lay out a hierarchy or breakdown of possible choices and outcomes?
* What decisions must be made?
* Which areas look as though they'll need the most time, the most energy?
  Which activities need careful scheduling or timing? What is the best scheduling and timing of them?
  Which parts will have the greatest impact if they succeed? If they fail? If they are delayed, disorganized, rearranged?
* Which parts must be kept in harmony with each other?

  Which parts could give each other support? Can this mutual benefit be arranged?
  In what political, organizational, ideological, or policy-oriented context will your solution be set? How will your solution fit into that context?

* Can you put into effect alternate plans and procedures if things go wrong?

Have you made specific plans for dealing with a particular kind of uncertainty?

* Must anything else happen to make your solution possible? What can you do to make sure it happens?

* What do you need in the way of people's time, materials, equipment, energy, coordination?

6-3. PREPARE IMPLEMENTATION PLANS.

* How do you plan to make your solution operate?

* Should you give this proposal a trial run before installing a full-scale solution?

Can you put your new idea in motion alongside the old situation to compare the two, to test the new idea, or to phase the new idea in gradually?

What actions and stages are required? How will you prevent these from becoming unsynchronized?

What will you do to make sure the separate parts of the project interlink smoothly?

* Have you a plan for assessing the solution's success?

Does everyone affected understand and accept the changes that might occur?

* How will you keep track of progress?

How will you keep an eye open for the unanticipated? What will you do?

7. Assess and improve your plans.

Since the situation is volatile, you ought to be sure your proposed solution has no flaws in it. You'll probably find some flaws when you look. Try to make a much better solution out of whatever you have (Micro-Strategy 13).

Is this solution what you really want? Is it really what is needed?

* Does it make a coherent whole, pattern, or explanation? Does it hang together properly?

* Can you find any loose ends? What are you going to do about them?

Could you take a broader outlook? Are you looking at the situation from too narrow a perspective?
* Are things really more complicated than this? Or simpler?
* Are you seriously considering more than one solution, or have you rushed for the one that seems to solve the most immediate aspects of the problem, or for the first appealing answer that sprang to mind?

Is anything within this solution at odds with itself?

Do any of the solution's objectives or procedures conflict with each other?

Are you avoiding the possibility that you should throw it all out and start again?

Will the solution have effects elsewhere?
* Is the solution moving on a collision course with anything else?

How might the solution be affected by something else connected with it?
* Have you considered what, if any, trade-offs may have to be made in selecting each alternative?
* What resources are used, what costs incurred, or what danger courted by each alternative solution?

* Can you find a way to make this solution more effective? More powerful? More significant?
* Can you find a way to make this solution simpler? Is there a simpler answer than this?

Can you find a way to solve the problem more quickly?
* Can you find a way to make the solution more flexible?
* Can you find a way to accomplish more with the same input?

Can the problem be solved using less energy, attention, or maintenance?

Could the solution produce more widespread or comprehensive benefits? What would be required to make this possible?

Could you combine the solution with another idea to produce something new?
* Can the best part of the solution be made better?

* Can the worst part be eliminated?
* Could you solve the problem in a bolder or more adventurous way?

  Can the solution be made less cumbersome, less involved, less tedious?

8. Reassess the immediate situation.

Don't relax your vigilance. Don't become overconfident. Unpredictable means just that. Something may yet stand you on your head. Keep watch for it. Think ahead imaginatively. If you take crisis action while using this section, or afterward, you may wish, before going on to the approach-choosing procedure in Section 6 or returning to the beginning of this strategy, to follow up your crisis action with a look at Micro-Strategy 24, "Taking stock," which should help you to assess the new situation.

* Has the situation changed? Must you take immediate action?

  Are any new patterns appearing? If so, what do they look like?

  Is there anything going on that may soon become part of your situation?

  Do you see any possible surprises on the way?

* Is anything falling behind? Is anything getting out of step? If so, what will the effects be? What will you do about it?
* If you can foresee something going wrong, how will you handle it, either to prevent it going wrong or to deal with it afterwards?

9. Take a wider look at the total situation.

See if you can get a better grasp of the total situation, its interrelationships and other intricacies, to the point that you really understand them (Micro-Strategy 15).

9-1. HOW DOES ALL THIS HANG TOGETHER?

How does each part interconnect or interact with other parts?

What is connected to what? Can you draw a map, diagram, flowchart or picture of the pieces? Can you see how each one is, or might be, connected to the others? Are there any missing connections?

Which interrelationships are close and strong? Which are loose and weak?

Which interrelationships are unchanging? Which ones change, fluctuate, become modified, or could do one of these things?

Which interrelationships seem clear and which are hard to fathom?

* Can you arrange the components and interrelationships in order of importance? Which part affects the greatest number of other parts? Which part has the strongest influence or effects?

* What other things might be connected to this problem, either directly or indirectly?

What is the nature or manner of these interactions?

How closely connected to the situation are these other subproblems, events, principles, functions, concepts?

Why are things interconnected or interacting in the ways that they are?

* How did the present relationships or arrangements of events become this way?

* How do quantities, values, arrangements, and characteristics change? What specific values do they assume?

* Can you identify and describe time scales, rhythms, or flows in activities or in the way this situation changes shape?

Do all these parts and functions form a coherent pattern? Do they all interact smoothly? Does the whole thing make sense?

* Is there a central area of complexity?

9-2. WHAT IS ALL THIS ABOUT?

What is this problem's place in the general scheme of things?

Do other systems, structures, or frameworks directly influence this situation? Are any ones influenced by it?

* Which parts, systems, persons, or events control, influence, or motivate others?

* How are any related or interacting situations developing? Look at other situations related to or interacting with the

main one. Look at related or interacting situations within the main one.

* What connections, interactions, traffic or interchange are there between this situation and its surroundings?
* How does the framework, institution, background, culture, or system that contains this problem interact with its surroundings? Can this interaction be changed?

Why is the context or framework containing this problem set up the way it is? What effects does this structure have on the problem? Can this be changed? Might it change anyway? What would happen if it did?

If you rearranged the surroundings of your problem, would the problem disappear?

* What assumptions are you making about the context of this situation? Are they valid?
* What holds everything together? What structures, processes, or people?

Does the situation lack harmony? Are things out of step, in conflict, at odds with each other, or out of balance?

* If there is a lack of harmony, is it reasonable? Couldn't it be changed? If so, in how many ways? If not, why not? And is the reason a real or sufficient one?

10. Return to the approach-choosing procedure.
Now that you have clarified the situation, you should be able to make a stronger attack on the problem as you perceive it. For assistance in preparing your plan of action, return to the approach-choosing procedure in Section 6.

Fuzzy

An essential part of dealing with fuzzy, obscure, or confusing situations is taking a look at everything from different angles. In this strategy you are directed by several routes toward finding original perspectives. You are forced to question assumptions and attitudes toward the problem. You are urged to hunt carefully and thoughtfully for information. The questions are intended to provoke an imaginative approach to your difficulties and to prompt you to restructure your view of the situation into new explanatory patterns. If your new perceptions reveal additional problems, you should follow the directions for mounting a new attack on the problem provided at the end of the strategy.

If your situation is extremely confusing, you may want to focus on your *objectives* when using this strategy. Your picture of what you are trying to achieve can shift as you learn more about a situation and detect new obstacles and opportunities.

After some section headings, micro-strategy numbers appear in parentheses. The micro-strategies referred to are suggestions for use, as a whole or in part, if you wish to expand the section. Using the micro-strategies in this way should enable you to adjust the emphasis of your strategy somewhat, depending on your circumstances and the size of the problem. For a fast route through the strategy, use only the questions marked with an asterisk.

For protection against frequent interruption, at intervals make a note of your position and ideas so that you won't forget them. The strategies are divided into segments to provide stopping points.

Outline of tasks

  1. The situation may be fuzzy, but you shouldn't be.
  2. Take a quick look at the situation.
  3. Examine ideas and concepts involved.
  4. Dig deeper.
  5. View the problem from other perspectives.
  6. Reflect upon what you have so far and pull it all together.
  7. Think about your new grasp of the situation.
  8. Return to the approach-choosing procedure.

1. The situation may be fuzzy but you shouldn't be.
Although your problem may look like a maze in the fog, you presumably have goals you want to achieve with it. Make sure these goals are clear enough that the elusive situation can't lead

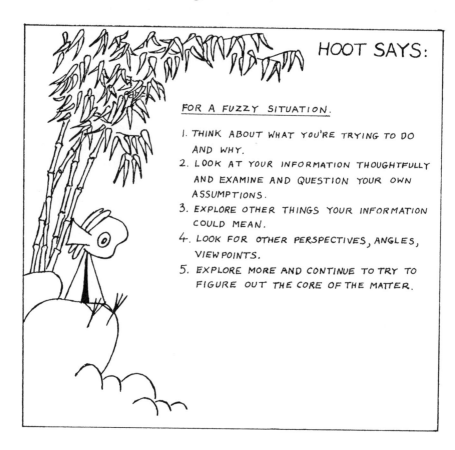

HOOT SAYS:

FOR A FUZZY SITUATION.

1. THINK ABOUT WHAT YOU'RE TRYING TO DO AND WHY.

2. LOOK AT YOUR INFORMATION THOUGHTFULLY AND EXAMINE AND QUESTION YOUR OWN ASSUMPTIONS.

3. EXPLORE OTHER THINGS YOUR INFORMATION COULD MEAN.

4. LOOK FOR OTHER PERSPECTIVES, ANGLES, VIEWPOINTS.

5. EXPLORE MORE AND CONTINUE TO TRY TO FIGURE OUT THE CORE OF THE MATTER.

you down a blind alley and leave you there. Be careful. The questions in this section demand thoughtful exploration.
* What are you trying to do? What issues are you struggling with? What do you hope to achieve?
* What, exactly, do you mean by that?
  What, exactly, do you mean by the answers you have just given to the last question?
* Are any of your objectives inconsistent or in conflict with each other?
  What does the situation you wish to bring about look like?
* Do you have alternative goals? If the route to one goal were blocked, could you take another direction?
* What will be the key signs of success? What will be the less important signs?
  What are your short-term or immediate goals?
  What are your longer-term or more distant goals?

2. Take a quick look at the situation.
A first exploration, more to raise questions than to answer them (Micro-Strategy 2).
* What do you already know about this situation?
* What could you quickly find out?
  What seem to be the objectives of this operation, framework, structure, or system? What purpose might it serve?
* What is this problem's place in the general scheme of things?
* What seem to be the main components and who seem to be the main participants of this problem? How many are there?
  What relationships do the main parts seem to have with each other?

  What can be inferred from what you have learned so far? What does this lead to?
* Can you see any contradictions or inconsistencies?
* Is there a core of organization or control, a main trouble spot, or a focus of confusion or puzzlement?
* Is there a technique, procedure, theory, principle, or concept already developed and available that would enable you to deal with this problem speedily and effectively?
* Is there a skill that you have, or that someone else you could

call upon has, that would enable you to deal with this problem speedily and effectively?
* Does your response to this question raise any deeper issues?

What hidden or unstated goals or directions might there be?
* What might be some of the long-term effects, influences, and interactions stemming from the components of this problem situation?
Have you considered what might happen outside the immediate problem area?
* Can you see any distinct patterns?
Might there be some other explanation of the problem?
Are things actually more complicated than this? Or simpler?
* What might you have missed?

3. Examine the ideas and concepts involved.

Now that you have some awareness of the range of the problem and its difficulties, or at least a general impression of the problem, start looking at the ideas and concepts that seem to be involved.

* What are the basic items or concepts that you are dealing with?
* What exactly do you understand by the terms, concepts, or ideas that you are dealing with, by the viewpoints you are expressing, by the questions you are asking?

   How are these words or ideas being used? What do they really mean? To you? To others?

   To what is each word or idea normally applied? How is it used?

   Are you using an idea, word, or phrase in different senses in different parts of your argument or concept, and thereby invalidating or weakening your conclusions or patterns?

   Does your usage, or normal usage, of this idea, concept, or word hide any inconsistencies, contradictions, or vagueness that should be pulled out and examined?

* Are you setting out with a completely wrong idea of what is, or should be, going on?

* Are you using an idea, word, or phrase in a different sense from that in which it is generally used? Have you acknowledged this?
* To what degree can this problem be solved, or a contribution to its solution be made, by process of argument, deduction, or putting together knowledge you already possess?
* To what degree can this problem be solved, or a contribution to its solution be made, by physical investigation, by empirical testing, by going and seeing?
* How could you restate your basic attitudes, assumptions, or ground rules to reveal any need there is for clarification, reformulation, or tidying up?
* Are any of the questions you are asking in this problem situation loaded or leading?

* Are you confusing any categories or types of things, mixing things that don't belong together, like apples and oranges, for example, which are sometimes different (one is citrus, the other not) and sometimes the same (both are fruit and grow on trees)?
* Which parts of this problem are objective or verifiable, and which are subjective, based in values, taste, opinion, or attitude?

   Could altering some of these values, attitudes, or opinions give you a different perspective?
* Is there a common thread running through all this, a central issue?

   Can you tease out and identify this central problem, or group of problems?

   How can you simplify the problem without oversimplifying it?

4. Dig deeper.

Now that you have some of your ideas and preconceptions sorted out a little better, dig deeper into the issue.

   What does the overall situation look like?
* What are the major trends? What are the minor trends? What do people think is going to happen?

   What are the most prominent, noteworthy, or urgent aspects of this problem? Why?

   Is this problem taking place within a larger system or problem, and closely interconnected with it?
* What seems to be happening? What larger difficulties are there, and what opportunities might there be?
* Why is all this taking place?

   Where is it all taking place?
   When is it occurring?
* How is it happening?
* What is the timing and how long do things last?
   How quickly are things happening?
   Who might be doing it?

* Who seems to be causing it?

How unpredictable is the situation? Is it completely uncertain, uncertain only within particular areas, or does it have some degree of probability?

* What seem to be the chief points to decide about or wrestle with?

* What procedures are being followed?

* What kinds of attitudes are involved?

What functions or operations seem to be involved?

What value systems or principles are involved?

* What and where are the weak, difficult, or tenuous points?

* What and where are the strong or secure points?

* Under what conditions or circumstances have observed events occurred or could they occur?

What conditions or circumstances would be required for the events under consideration to occur?

What factors or considerations are or could have been responsible for changes in the direction of the events under investigation?

What might you have missed?

* Can you benefit from others who have experienced similar situations? What did they learn? How can you find out?

Can you find out what has been said about this problem, done about it, written about it?

* Can you draw a parallel from the past?

Is there a place or person anywhere in the world that could help you with a situation like this? Can you go there? Can you contact the person?

* How did the present relationships or arrangements of events become this way?

* Can you see patterns of growth, change, decay or evolution? What seem to be the significant events, trends, people, and influences involved?

Look at the historical path of this situation. Does the way things have developed tell you that some ways of tackling the problem might be a waste of time?

5. View the problem from other perspectives.

Don't let the information you've accumulated obscure other issues. Try to see things from some other perspectives (Micro-Strategies 9 and 10).

* Is there another way you could look at this situation that might throw a different light on it? That is, could the problem be seen as part of a different issue? Could it be seen as an opportunity in disguise, as a chance to get something different straightened out? Try hard to look at it in different ways.

    What other process, problem, or situation resembles this one in some way?

* Who could give you another outlook or angle on this situation?

If you had a different occupation, how might this problem
   look to you?
* What is the most appealing, noteworthy, interesting, or useful aspect of this? Can you use it to find a new angle?
* How can you modify the scope or boundaries of this problem? Expand it? Contract it? Could doing this help to provide a fresh perspective?

* What does the problem look like from the other end? Can you
   turn the situation on its head?
   Is there anything inappropriate about what you are doing?
   About your expectations concerning results, your own behavior, the behavior of others, the future, capacities, capabilities?
   Maybe you have all this back to front?
   How can you take a viewpoint that would make things look
   different?
* Can you take a different starting point?
* Are you looking at this problem in different ways, on different levels? Have you considered aspects such as organization, esthetics, personality, timing, information, motivation, effort, production, finance? What other vantage points
   for looking at the problem can you think of?
   Why do you see this as a problem? What objectives are not
   being achieved?
* What personal, psychological, emotional blockages or blind
   spots in yourself or others may be involved?

* What might happen next? In the near future? In the long
   term?
* Can you see a reason why the future of this situation would
   differ considerably from the past?
   How might future developments affect this situation?
   What else could you make of all this?
* Can you look at this problem from a different angle, for ex-
   ample, from an emotional, geographical, rational, personal,
   chronological, political, or ethical one?
   Have you come across other situations like this one?

* Look out the window. Let the first thing you see set your thoughts about the problem on a new path.

6. Reflect upon what you have so far and pull it all together (Micro-Strategies 11, 8, 26, and 13).

Which bits and pieces do you think are relevant?

* What seem to be the key points in this situation? What are the critical aspects?
* Where are all the pertinent, relevant ideas and information that you have so far? Can you gather them together?
* Out of this material can you extract what seem to be the central issues?

Can you clarify things by arranging the ideas or information around these central issues?

* How do you think all this fits together? Have you a first guess, a hunch to test out?
* Is there a pattern you can pick out, invent, or borrow from somewhere else that could explain this?
* What can you find to synthesize or integrate all this? Would an old idea fit? Or must you find something new?

* Can you see any distinct patterns?

What are the objectives of this operation, situation, structure, or system?

* What different kinds of interpretations can you think of?
* What is connected to what? Can you draw a map, diagram, flowchart, or picture of your main facts? Can you see how each one is, or should be, connected to the others? Are there any missing connections?
* Are there any intriguing coincidences?

Could you use your new idea, concept, viewpoint, metaphor, or synthesis more effectively?

Does this synthesis, viewpoint, or metaphor explain only the current situation? Or does it make new predictions, generate new hypotheses, and open up new, fruitful avenues for exploration?

7. Think about your grasp of the situation (Micro-Strategy 15).
* Does any information you have at hand show that the situation is really not what it seems?
* Are you sure you have all the information you need to figure this out?

   Have your "facts" been confirmed or supported by additional sources?
* Have you thought this through really thoroughly?
* Do your ideas form a coherent whole or pattern?
* Can you see loose ends? Why?

   Are you looking at the situation from too narrow a perspective? Are you making any assumptions that you should perhaps question, for example, with regard to the environment, political aspects, personal factors, technological aspects, present trends, economic aspects, skills, training, policy, or organization?

   Are the value systems, beliefs, or attitudes that you are assuming to be operating in this situation really there? Could this change? What would be the effects?
* Could someone be misleading you? Accidentally? Deliberately?
* Are there other ideas that draw the opposite or different conclusions from your idea?

   What do you make of that?

   Has your idea solved the problem, or transferred it, or hidden it?
* Are you afraid to consider the possibility of having to throw it all out and start again?

8. Return to the approach-choosing procedure.
Now that you have clarified the situation, you should be able to make a stronger attack on the problem as you perceive it. For assistance in preparing your plan of attack, return to the approach-choosing procedure in Section 6.

Complex, Unpredictable, and Fuzzy

Pressure usually accompanies complicated and uncertain conditions. Consequently, this strategy is more compact than the attributes complexity, unpredictability, and fuzziness might seem to require. The procedure is intended to guide you quickly toward cleaning up the complexity and obscurity, while helping you plan for crises. You are encouraged to use a blend of careful analysis and imaginative speculation in dealing with the complications and uncertainties.

After some section headings, micro-strategy numbers appear in parentheses. The micro-strategies referred to are suggestions for use, as a whole or in part, if you wish to expand the section. Using the micro-strategies in this way should enable you to adjust the emphasis of your strategy somewhat, depending on your circumstances and the size of the problem. For a fast route through the strategy, use only the questions marked with an asterisk.

For protection against frequent interruption, at intervals make a note of your position and ideas so that you won't forget them. The strategies are divided into segments to provide stopping points.

Outline of tasks
1. Prepare for crisis.
2. Set objectives.
    2-1.Keep your eyes open.
3. Seek information.
4. Take a more thorough look around.
5. Reassess the immediate situation.

6. Plan.
 6-1. Collect the pieces.
 6-2. Construct the plan.
7. Reassess.
 7-1. Reassess the immediate situation.
 7-2. Reconsider the problem.
 7-3. Check out your solution.
8. Act.
9. Take stock.

1. Prepare for crisis.
In case the unpredictable happens, you should have some kind of contingency plan. Work through this section in order to think out your response to emergency.
* What *must* be rescued or protected to guarantee survival of basic functions and purposes? Are there any fundamentally important areas?
* Can you reduce the range of issues requiring your immediate attention? What is vital to survival?
* Can you tease out, identify, and tackle a central need, activity, or function, or group of these? What is the crux of this matter?
* What is the least that *must* be done?
* How will you cope with any emergency you can predict? How will you organize things? What steps will you take?

2. Set objectives.
Clarify what you are trying to achieve and the direction you hope to move in (Micro-Strategy 2).
* What are you trying to do? What issues are you struggling with? What do you hope to achieve?
* Do any of your objectives conflict with each other? Are there any inconsistencies?
  What does the situation you wish to bring about look like?
  What will be your signs of success? How will you decide when you have resolved things?
* If you can reach only some of your objectives, what will be your priorities?

2-1. KEEP YOUR EYES OPEN.

To become more flexible and adaptable in your responses, you need information to help you predict what will happen next. Stay watchful.

* What information will you need to remain aware of what is happening?

    How will you be able to see, predict, or find out about what will happen next?

    How will you decide what your information or news indicates?

* How will you decide whether you should act, and what action you might take?

3. Seek information.

Figure out what the real issues are. Don't set off with only a vague and hasty perception of the problem (Micro-Strategies 1 and 7).

* What do you already know? What information is immediately available?

* What could you quickly find out?

* What seems to be happening? What difficulties does this cause? What opportunities does this lead to?

    Where does it all seem to be happening?

    When is it happening?

    How is it taking place?

* How are things timed? How long do they take?

    How fast are things happening?

* Why is it all occurring?

    Who seems to be doing it?

    Who might be causing it?

    What does the overall situation look like?

* Which seem to be the main centers of trouble, or the potential trouble spots?

* What are the components and who are the participants of this problem? How many are there?

* What are the most critical, noteworthy, or urgent aspects of this problem? Why?

* How complicated does the problem seem to be? How many parts, levels, or divisions does it seem to have?
* How has this problem developed?
  How long has this been going on?

  How do you know your information is correct and unbiased?
* What remains to be learned? What are you unsure of?
* What are the areas where confusion or fuzziness or difficulty are being found, or seem likely to be found?
  Can you make a first guess, however rough, at the nature of the various difficulties?
  Can you make some other guesses, some other interpretations?
  What are the basic items or concepts that you are dealing with?

* What do you understand by the terms, concepts, or ideas that you are dealing with, by the viewpoints you are expressing, by the questions you are asking?
* Are you confusing any categories or types of things, mixing things that don't belong together, like apples and oranges, for example, which are sometimes different (one is citrus, the other not) and sometimes the same (both are fruit and grow on trees)?
* Can you see any decisive patterns in growth or change rates or directions, in components or factors, or in their interrelationships?
  Might you find a pattern by altering your viewpoint or changing your expectations of this situation?
  Who could help you with this by offering you a new perspective?
  Are you allowing yourself to relax and be open to different interpretations?

4. Take a more thorough look around.
As we have noted, in this strategy you are alternating between preparing more carefully for crisis, emergency, or sudden change, and trying to determine the roots of the unpredictabil-

ity in your situation. Here, the activity is seeking out and examining the unpredictability.

* How can you find out about the unpredictability, threat, or competition? Is there someone you can talk to about it, somewhere you could look for information, something you could read, remember, see?

  Can you find the source of the unpredictability, threat, or competition?

* From where and from how many sources is the unpredictability coming? Where else might it develop?

  Can you isolate the unpredictable part of the situation and stay clear of it, or minimize its impact?

* Who or what is, or might be, causing unpredictability? Now? In the future?

* What significant new directions could alter the kinds of, and sources of, unpredictability? Where are the areas of accelerating growth?

  Where is the power to change things (other than yourself) located? What is the source of power doing?

* What else is going on? Is it significant? Could you connect this other thing going on to your situation either by discovering subtle links or by making an innovation?

* If you can foresee something going wrong, do you have a way of handling it or preventing it?

* What would happen if the problem situation suddenly improved, or deteriorated?

  Can you see a reason why the future of this situation might differ considerably from the past?

5. Reassess the immediate situation.

Keep your eyes open. Stay alert. Make sure you get as much warning as possible of impending shifts in the situation (Micro-Strategy 21).

* Has the situation changed? Must you take immediate action?

  Does the situation look as though it is changing or about to change?

  Has the situation already changed in a manner that's hard to

recognize? Is it different even though it seems the same?
Has the situation remained fundamentally the same despite
apparent changes?
* In what way that would surprise you can you imagine the
situation changing? What might happen? What might be
your weakest spot?
What could you do to be ready for this?
* Must you now reorganize, rearrange, or reschedule any part
of the current effort? Must you change priorities, expand,
or contract?

6. Plan.
Pull together imaginatively and carefully all the pieces of this
puzzle and develop some equally imaginative and careful action
plans to resolve your difficulties.

6-1. COLLECT THE PIECES (MICRO-STRATEGIES 26 AND 11).
* How can you break the situation down into its sub-problems?
How are the components tied together? Closely, loosely, at
all?
* What is overlapping with what? What is interacting with
what? What is feeding back into what?
What parts are conflicting with each other? What ideas, feelings, attitudes, requirements, concepts, functions, or components are colliding with each other?
* Can you tease out, identify, and tackle a central problem, or
group of problems?

* What interactions are there among sub-problems?
* What interactions are there between the sub-problems and
the overall situation? What part does each play in the
whole?
* What interactions are there between the overall problem and
surrounding events? What part does the problem play in its
context?
* Can you solve and assess the solution of each sub-problem
using 6-2 and 7 in this strategy?
* Can you examine and piece together all the sub-problem solutions using 6-2 and 7 in this strategy to produce a coherent, coordinated solution?

6-2. CONSTRUCT THE PLAN (MICRO-STRATEGIES 9, 10, 12, AND 13).

What is happening in the short term that you know you must deal with?

* What are the things that you must do? Make a detailed list of these actions.

* What are these actions a part of? Where do they fit? What links to what else?

What will happen in the long term that you will have to deal with?

Can you divide these activities or events into different areas, groups, or types of activities or problems?

* How are these detailed actions related to your larger objectives? Which larger objectives is each detailed action designed to further?

* What are your overall objectives? What are the steps along the way? What intermediate goals must you reach to achieve these objectives?
* What activities are required for you to achieve your objectives or your intermediate goals?
* Can you break these objectives and intermediate goals down into more detailed activity requirements?

  Can you lay out a flowchart, hierarchy, or breakdown of sub-problems, sub-components, or decisions to be made?

  Can you lay out a flowchart, hierarchy, or breakdown of possible choices and outcomes?

  Which activities are critical to survival? Which activities support your important goals?
* What priorities do the various tasks have? Can you rate them in order of importance?

  Which parts interlock or harmonize?
* Which activities need careful scheduling or timing? What is the best scheduling and timing of them?

* Can you look into the future and see anything that might thwart your plans?
* What might you have missed? Is there any area you haven't thought about?

  Can you produce an overall picture that shows clearly how all the pieces fit together?
* Can you develop other routes to your overall objectives, by establishing other intermediate goals, for example, so that when one route is blocked another might still be open?

  How many alternate routes to your goals can you develop?
* Can you now develop a preferred plan and a couple of backup plans?

7. Reassess.

Don't relax your vigilance. Don't become overconfident. Events around you, your interpretation of the situation, or flaws in the solution you have chosen, may turn the world upside down. Be on your guard.

7-1. REASSESS THE IMMEDIATE SITUATION.

* Has the situation changed? Must you take immediate action?
  Are any new patterns emerging? If so, what do they look like?
  Is there anything going on that may soon become part of your
    situation?
  Can you foresee any surprises on the way?
* Is anything falling behind? Is anything getting out of step? If
  so, what will the effect be? What will you do about it?
* If you can foresee something going wrong, how will you han-
  dle it, either to prevent it going wrong, or to deal with it
  afterwards?

7-2. RECONSIDER THE PROBLEM.

  Why do you see this as a problem? What objectives are not
    being achieved?
* Are you setting out with a completely wrong idea of what is,
  or should be, going on?
* Do you have any information at hand that might reveal the
  situation to be not what it seems?
  Is there anything that is so much a part of the accepted way
    of looking at things that it cannot be seen as an issue?
* Have you really grasped what is happening?

* Are you unsure of or suspicious of any of your information?
  If so, check it out carefully. Does your new information lead
  to different interpretations?
  Have your facts been confirmed or supported by additional
    sources or means?
  What remains to be learned? What are you unsure of?
* Who could give you another outlook on this situation?

  What other things does your interpretation of the situation
    imply or lead to? Can you find evidence to support these
    implications? Do your efforts lead to new avenues of in-
    quiry?
  How many interpretations can you think of?
* Does considering other interpretations raise deeper issues?
* Are things really more complicated than this, or simpler?

Can you see any clear patterns?

* Are there any intriguing coincidences?
  Is there a center of complexity?
* Which part of your problem causes the most difficulty and why?
  Have you checked out even the most obvious aspects of the situation?
* Can you see contradictions or inconsistencies?
  Do you have all this upside down?

If you want to replan your approach at this point, and your problem is not too large, return to 6 in this strategy. If you feel no need to replan, then proceed to 7-3, "Checking out your solution." If your problem is fairly large, you may want to work through the following questions first.

FOR LARGE PROBLEMS ONLY.
* What are you trying to pin down? What do your intuitions or hunches say?
* What is puzzling you?
  Is this problem too involved or difficult for you to deal with alone?
  How complicated does this problem seem to be? How many parts, sections, levels, or divisions does it seem to have?
* How much problem-solving effort does this situation merit?
* What is this problem's place in the general scheme of things?
  Is there a bigger problem that contains this one? Should you tackle that?
  Are you trying to discover the truth here, or trying to find what you would like to find?
* What is distinctive or special about this operation or situation? How can you accommodate this special quality or take advantage of it?
  At what level or from what direction would this problem best be approached?

* How can you get the most out of solving this problem?

How might future developments affect this system?
* Is this situation also caught up in other kinds of difficulties?
  Must you look outside the immediate situation to discover
  the objectives or the motivating or controlling forces?
* What hidden or unstated directions or goals might there be?
  Is the justification for this system to be found outside the
  present circumstances?

Now return to 6 of this strategy to replan, if this seems necessary. Otherwise, carry on to 7-3.

7-3. CHECK OUT YOUR SOLUTION.
* Is your solution doomed from the start?
  Is this solution what you really want? Is it what is really nec-
  essary?
* Where do you see the greatest risks? What are the greatest
  challenges? Can these be handled?
* Can you see loose ends? If so, what will you do about them?
  Is any part of the solution in conflict with, at odds with, or
  inconsistent with, another part?

* Can you see contradictions or inconsistencies anywhere?
* Are you seriously considering more than one solution? Or
  have you rushed for the one that seems to solve the most
  immediate aspects of the problem, or seems most appealing?
* Have you researched this problem thoroughly?
  Is the solution really as novel or innovative as you think?
  Is it really as comprehensive or all-encompassing as you
  think?

Might you have to throw it all out and start again?
* Are there other ideas that resemble your idea, or that have
  been put in effect to deal with your concerns? How does
  your idea compare with these other ideas?
* Are there other ideas that draw the opposite or different conclusions from your idea? What do you make of that?
  Has anyone gone any further than you with this problem?

How? Why?
* Has your idea solved the problem, transferred it, or hidden it?
* How will you make your solution operate properly in its transition from paper to life?
    Have you planned and organized the implementation properly?
* What steps, phases, or stages are required? What will you do if these become unsynchronized?

If you want to replan your approach at this point, and your problem is not too large, return to 6 in this strategy. If you feel no need to replan, then proceed to 8, "Act." If your problem is fairly large, you may want to work through the following questions first.

FOR LARGE PROBLEMS ONLY.
* Will this solution have effects elsewhere?
* Is the solution moving on a collision course with anything else?
* How might this plan be affected by other things connected with it?
    Can you see when and why these things might occur?
    How might these things happen and with what results?
    What would you do if these things did happen?

* Have you looked at the various solutions proposed to see what, if any, trade-offs might have to be made for each?
* If each of your solutions has several possible outcomes, and you cannot decide which solution is best, can you decide which solution contains the outcome that would be the worst, and reject this one?
* What resources are used, what costs incurred, or what danger courted by each alternative solution?
    Can you see who might develop, grow, or benefit as a result of this situation?
    Who might suffer as a result of this situation?

* Have you looked at what might happen outside the immedi-

ate problem area?
* What duration, cost, urgency, potential, and priority does each part of your plan have?
  Can you foresee future developments that might have a bad effect on your solution?
  When you consider the future of each part of your solution, do things remain in the same arrangement? If not, will your solution still work?
* If you can foresee anything going wrong, can you think of a way to handle it?
  Can you think of any crises or disasters that could affect your solution? How would you prevent or handle them?

Now return to 6 of this strategy to replan, if this seems necessary. Otherwise, move on to 8.

8. Act.
Should you act now? If so, take action and then consider the results of your action by responding to the questions in 9 in this strategy. If you do not plan to act now, you may wish to return to 7 to spend more time reassessing or to 4 to dig deeper for information (Micro-Strategy 19).

9. Take stock.
Now look at your progress. Can you do even better? Can you remedy mistakes? What can you learn from your experiences? (Micro-Strategy 20).
  Are you achieving your overall objectives?
* Have your actions had the required effects? If not, why did they fail? How long did things survive, and why?
  If you failed, did this give you any new wisdom, insights, or perceptions?
  If you succeeded, can you improve upon your success?
* Have your actions or their effects revealed new opportunities? If so, what can be done to exploit these?

* Have you really been effective, or are appearances deceiving you?
  Did something just happen or change? If so, will it have any

effect or not? Where does it fit? What could be done about it?

* Should you implement your crisis plan? Do you have a crisis plan? If not, work through Micro-Strategy 6 to devise one.
* Imagine that the situation, events, or participants are conspiring to surprise you. What would be your weakest spot? What might happen?

What could you do to be ready for this?

* What else is going on? Is it significant? Could you connect your situation with this other thing going on, either by discovering subtle links, or by making an innovation?

What would happen if the problem situation suddenly deteriorated? What if it suddenly improved?

* Can you see the situation a lot more clearly now? Does one of the new viewpoints make you want to try a new and better solution or a new and better approach?

Are there any new problems that need to be solved? If so, how will you tackle them?

* Should you reorganize, rearrange, or reschedule any part of the current effort? Should you change priorities, expand, or contract?
* Did you work in the most effective way? Was this the best action you could have taken?

Did you try to cut out activities that did not contribute directly to overall objectives? Did you concentrate on activities that did?

* Do your experiences show how you could improve your problem-solving methods to produce better solutions faster in the future?

Crisis

In a crisis situation, some major part of life is being endangered. Often this threat has such an emotional impact that you become frantic with worry and unable to help yourself. Your company or your marriage may be falling apart and putting grave strain on everything you've worked for, hoped for, and believed in. Or, some civil or environmental disaster may be threatening the roots of your existence.

In all cases, being prepared for crisis is the best means of surviving it. Avoiding complacency and continually trying to grow in an aware and thoughtful manner is the key to heading off most crises in business and personal relationships and to surviving a cataclysm such as an earthquake or a flood.

The worst crises of your life will be the ones that take you by surprise. At these times you will be called upon to put out a supreme effort under the worst conditions, often with yourself as your worst enemy. In such cases the best you can do is to try to identify—at this stage probably by feel or instinct—what *must* survive, and then try to rescue it at whatever cost. If what you want to rescue is the most important thing in the world to you, it will be worthwhile to sacrifice lesser objectives if necessary.

The next stage is critical. Once you have saved what is basic to your existence—your life, family, career, business, marriage, or whatever—you must pull yourself together as quickly as possible and begin to work on the situation to ensure the *continued* survival of this fundamental piece of your life. See what you can do to gain time, to gain a breathing space. See what can be done to avoid future crisis. Only when you have secured the fundamentals should you turn to lesser objectives. Don't relax too soon and lose it all. Before you set out with this strategy, consider the following two points.

Do you really have a crisis?
First be sure that you really have a crisis. It's easy to lose perspective on a situation by focusing on a small range of events and failing to see the overall picture. These small things then take on an exaggerated importance. They should be cut back down to size.

So, when you are faced with an apparent crisis, take a quick look at what else is happening, or what else has happened. By making sure that you have things in perspective and that the

HOOT SAYS:

FOR A CRISIS SITUATION

1. FIGURE OUT WHAT THE ABSOLUTE BASICS ARE AND MAKE A PLAN TO RESCUE OR PROTECT THESE.
2. IF YOU CAN, OR IF THERE'S TIME, MAKE A PLAN TO RESCUE MORE THAN JUST THE BASICS.
3. IF YOU CAN, OR IF THERE'S TIME, TRY TO TURN THIS CRISIS INTO SOMETHING WHOSE BENEFITS WILL FAR OUTWEIGH ITS DISASTROUS ASPECTS.

apparent crisis is set in its proper context, you can avoid panic. Otherwise you may *precipitate* crisis by generating a critical situation out of a merely difficult one. Occasionally things can improve after being brought to a head, because that way the matter can't be avoided any longer. But this occurrence is more an exception than a rule. A life of continuing crisis will finally defeat the best of us.

Do you think you're OK?

One defense against the worst effects of crisis is to remind yourself that you are a worthwhile person. Many of us are too hard on ourselves, don't think we can do things, don't believe we deserve to succeed, always look on the black side, and expect only the worst. Usually these are self-fulfilling prophecies. We say we can't do it, so we don't. We expect failure, so we get it. We don't think we are worthwhile, so we gradually erode our confidence and eventually destroy ourselves, or at least make sure we are just mediocre instead of special. All of us are unique and special in our own right. This makes it OK to be us, even though we may—and usually do—have problems to work on. The confidence and optimism that goes with feeling OK about yourself is a tremendous weapon in combating crisis and disaster. It also helps you to arrange your life-style so that some crises just don't occur. If you are one of the innumerable people who feel really down on themselves, start to work on feeling that it's OK to be you. This will make life a warmer place and problems and crises much less dangerous. Just try it. You may be pleasantly surprised.

This strategy is focused on the basics. What *must* survive, and how can this survival be guaranteed? A positive attitude is also encouraged and a section is included to explore the possibility that your misfortune may contain the seeds of new opportunities. Don't forget: If you find yourself getting into further trouble, make use of the HELP sections, starting at Section 12.

After some section headings, micro-strategy numbers appear in parentheses. The micro-strategies referred to are suggestions for use, as a whole or in part, if you wish to expand the section. Using the micro-strategies in this way should enable you to adjust the emphasis of your strategy somewhat, depending on your circumstances and the size of the problem. For a fast route through the strategy, use only the questions marked with an asterisk.

For protection against frequent interruption, at intervals make a note of your position and ideas so that you won't forget them. The strategies are divided into segments to provide stopping points.

Outline of tasks
1. What must be rescued or protected?
2. How might this be done?
3. Reassess the immediate situation.
4. What new opportunities does this catastrophe offer?
5. Take the next steps.

1. What must be rescued or protected?
Act to guarantee survival of basic functions and purposes (Micro-Strategy 2).

FIRST LOOK.
What activities, functions, people, items, or relationships must you preserve or rescue?
What is required to do this?
How might you accomplish this?

KEEP YOUR EYES OPEN.
To become more flexible and adaptable in your responses, you need information to help you predict what might happen. Information and flexibility are important in all strategies. In crisis they are *vital*. So, stay watchful.
What information will you need to remain aware of what is happening?
How will you see, predict, or find out about what might happen next?
How will you decide what your information or news indicates?
How will you decide whether you should act, and what action you should take?

SECOND LOOK.

What gives meaning to your life or operation? What do you
care deeply about? Is there a higher objective or principle
that could guide you? Can you use this as a focus?
Can you reduce the range of issues requiring your immediate
attention? What is vital to survival?
Can you tease out, identify, and tackle a central need, activity, or function, or group of these? What is the crux of this
matter?

Are you sure you have the situation straight? Is the crisis
really rooted where you think it is?
Are there any fundamentally important areas?
What is the least you *must* do?
What is the most you *can* do?
What might happen next?

2. How might this be done?
Get organized—and fast. Get ready for action (Micro-Strategies
4 and 19).

What seem to be the critical areas?
Can you pull out one problem to focus on, and get started?
Is there a technique, procedure, theory, concept, agency, or
principle already developed and available that would enable you to deal with this problem speedily and effectively?
Is there a skill that you have, or that someone you can call
upon has, that would enable you to deal with this problem
speedily and effectively?

What sequence of actions is required? What timing is required?
Which activities would have the greatest impact if they were
unsuccessful? If they were delayed? If they succeeded? If
they were rearranged or disorganized?
If you can see anything that might suddenly become vital, is
there a way of handling it?
How can you push this action through fast?
What will you do in case of another emergency? How will you

act? What arrangements will you make?

3. Reassess the immediate situation.

Keep your eyes open. Stay alert. Make sure you get as much warning as possible of impending shifts in the situation (Micro-Strategy 21).

Has the situation changed? Must you implement your crisis plan? If so, execute your plan and then return to the approach-choosing procedure in Section 6 to examine the new situation. If you are not implementing your crisis plan, proceed with the following questions.

Does the situation look as though it is changing or about to change?

Has the situation already changed in a manner that's hard to recognize?

Is the situation different even though it seems the same?

Has the situation remained fundamentally the same despite apparent changes?

In what ways that would surprise you can you imagine the situation changing? What would be your weakest spot? What might happen?

What could you do to be ready for this?

Must you now reorganize, rearrange, or reschedule any part of the current effort? Must you change priorities, expand, or contract? If so, you may wish to return to 2 of this strategy or you may wish to work through Micro-Strategy 3, "Getting organized."

4. What new opportunities does this catastrophe offer?

Despite the apparent difficulty or disaster, does the situation still offer some opportunity to turn everything to your advantage? (Micro-Strategies 23, 9, 10, and 25).

Is there another way you could look at this situation that might throw a different light on it? That is, could the situation be seen as part of a different issue? Could it be seen as an opportunity in disguise, as a chance to get something different straightened out? Try hard to look at the situation in different ways.

Are there any intriguing coincidences?

Can you think of another explanation of the problem?

What else might you be able to make out of the problem?

Can you find someone to give you another outlook on the situation?

What might a blacksmith, a doctor, or a sailor have to say about this?

How would the French, the Italians, or the Russians deal with this?

What is the most intriguing, challenging, appealing, or useful aspect of the problem? Can you use it to find a new angle?

Can you change the scope or boundaries of this problem? Can you extend it or restrict it? Could this help you to tackle the problem more effectively?

What indirect approach can you take with this problem? What unexpected angles could you try?

What does the problem look like from the other end or from the other side? Can you turn the situation on its head?

Can you see the humorous side of the situation? Could a more relaxed frame of mind lead to a stronger attack upon the problem, or give you some hints?

5. Take the next steps.

Now take action. As soon as you feel you are out of the immediate crisis situation, but still in need of problem-solving support, return to the approach-choosing procedure in Section 6 to begin another attack on your difficulties.

Intractable

Everything is continuously in flux in an intractable situation. The parts involved are not easily managed or manipulated. They change, expand, and contract. The relationships between these parts also change. In addition, the rate and direction of development of the overall situation keeps fluctuating, so that everywhere things seem unpredictable.

For the turbulent and chaotic conditions of an intractable situation, just the barest bones of a strategy can be provided. No one posture can be adhered to. As you work with your problems, you will have to change the strategy continually. Hence, this strategy contains only an outline procedure, consisting of a few groups of core questions. The principal task is to LEARN about the situation, and to try to devise means of learning as fast and effectively as possible.

Battling with an intractable situation is the first stage in a process of struggling toward greater awareness and competence. Eventually in this process the difficulties should be reduced to the point where a slightly more structured approach like Strategy 6, "Complex, Fuzzy, and Unpredictable," could be used. Progressively, the problems should be defined more and more clearly, and more assured efforts made to solve them. The level of the difficulties should be gradually reduced from *intractable* to *complex* and *unpredictable*, and then to *large* or *medium* and *straightforward*. Thus, the strategy for an intractable situation is just the begining.

In approaching an intractable situation, or any problem situation, you should bear in mind that thoughtless or ill-considered action can turn a straightforward or complex situation into a chaotic and turbulent one. Human history is littered with incidents in which the participants suddenly find that they have a tiger by the tail.

Here are a few guidelines to keep in mind as you approach your turbulent situation.

—At every stage avoid irrevocable acts, that is, acts that commit you to something inflexible. Try to ensure that each action allows you a couple of outs, so that in some manner or other you can recover from your actions.

—You are exploring areas for which, by definition, no predetermined methodologies exist. You must be prepared to rebuild continually. Your knowledge, expectations, and actions will need constant modification.

—Hunt for allegories or metaphors as part of your pattern

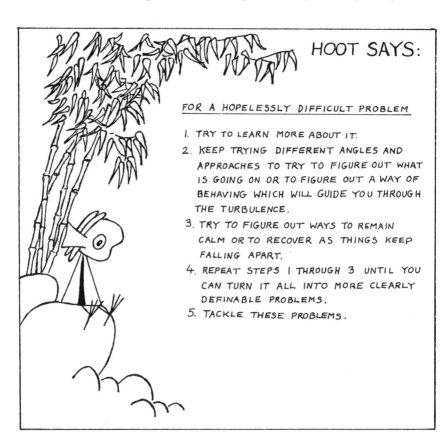

HOOT SAYS:

FOR A HOPELESSLY DIFFICULT PROBLEM

1. TRY TO LEARN MORE ABOUT IT.

2. KEEP TRYING DIFFERENT ANGLES AND APPROACHES TO TRY TO FIGURE OUT WHAT IS GOING ON OR TO FIGURE OUT A WAY OF BEHAVING WHICH WILL GUIDE YOU THROUGH THE TURBULENCE.

3. TRY TO FIGURE OUT WAYS TO REMAIN CALM OR TO RECOVER AS THINGS KEEP FALLING APART.

4. REPEAT STEPS 1 THROUGH 3 UNTIL YOU CAN TURN IT ALL INTO MORE CLEARLY DEFINABLE PROBLEMS.

5. TACKLE THESE PROBLEMS.

seeking, and do so imaginatively.

—You are striving to increase your information about what is going on, and what might happen next. Even if your actions seem to fail, make sure that you learn as much as possible from them.

—Look ahead. Attempt to extend "visible," predictable time, to give yourself more room for maneuver and to bring the situation under control gradually.

—Review is valuable not only to see what happened when you did what you did, and to provide a base for deciding where you might go next, but also for keeping things together, for avoiding fragmentation of effort.

—Keep a record of things you try and what happened. You're bound to make some mistakes anyway, so why make the same ones twice?

—Don't forget that since you, too, are an actor in the situation, you will be an influence on the events and their interpretation. You may change it all yourself.

Note that the following strategy is made up of micro-strategies. You can make up your own strategies for intractable situations, if you wish, by using micro-strategies from the list in the table of contents.

For protection against frequent interruption, at intervals make a note of your position and ideas so that you won't forget them. The strategies are divided into segments to provide stopping points.

Outline of tasks
   1. What's going on?
   2. What patterns are there?
   3. What might you try next?
   4. Act.
   5. What do you know now?
   6. Recommence the cycle.

1. What's going on?
   What do you already know about this situation? What could you quickly find out?
   Where else could you find information about this?

What sources that you've never thought of or heard of, or that you have previously considered and rejected might you turn to now?

What outlandish possibilities are there? Could these be turned to good account?

What might happen next? In the short term? In the long term?

What different shapes might the future take? How might these be provoked? What information would indicate that these directions are being taken?

Are you looking far enough ahead?

What must you do to unearth, detect, or develop information about areas of accelerating growth; evolutionary, developmental, or historical patterns for the overall situation and/or separate parts; interactions between parts, people, factors, and attitudes; things that are part of all this and things that are not, and things that sometimes are and sometimes aren't.

What seem to be the significant events, trends, persons, and influences involved?

Is there any way to pool resources or effort with anyone else working on the same or a similar problem?

Is there anywhere close by that you could go to learn about a problem like this? Can you contact people there? Could they help?

Where is the best place in the world for getting help with a problem like this? Can you go there? Can you contact people there? Could they help?

How do you know you have or could obtain accurate and unbiased information?

Can your "facts" be confirmed or supported by additional sources or means?

Are you looking at information or ideas not just for what theories they seem to support but also for what theories they do *not* support?

Are you doing everything possible to get a current and accurate picture?

What might you have missed?

At this point you may feel it would help to turn to Micro-Strategy 6, "Making a crisis plan."

2. What patterns are there?

Are there any odd or intriguing coincidences?

Can you reduce the range of issues requiring your immediate attention? What is vital to survival? Can you find a focus?

Is there a common thread running through all the parts of this problem? Are all or many of these parts related in some way?

Can you tease out, identify, and tackle a central problem, or group of problems?

Might you find some pattern by altering your viewpoint or changing your expectations of this situation?

What hidden or unstated directions, goals, requirements, or needs might there be?

Might someone be misleading you? Accidentally? Deliberately?

What is the most outstanding, noteworthy, appealing, or useful aspect of this situation? Can you use it to find a new angle?

What does the problem look like from the other end or from the other side? Can you turn the situation on its head?

Is there an aspect of the problem that is so much a part of the accepted way of looking at things that it is likely to be overlooked, or not seen as being a possible factor or issue?

Are any of your expectations unrealistic or out of place, for instance, expectations concerning results, your behavior, the behavior of others, the future, capacities, or capabilities?

Might you find a pattern by delving into fundamental assumptions, beliefs, concepts, or values with which you are approaching this situation and/or life in general? Can you examine the context in which you are setting all this?

Can you see any clear or possible patterns in growth or change rates and directions, in components or factors, or in their interrelationships?

What are the basic items, assumptions, beliefs, or concepts that you are dealing with?

What do you understand by the terms or concepts you are using, by the viewpoints you are expressing, by the questions you are asking?

How could you restate your basic attitudes, assumptions, or ground rules to reveal the need for clarification, reformulation, or tidying up?

Which parts of this problem are objective or verifiable and which are subjective, based in values, taste, opinion, or attitude?

Is there another way you could look at this situation that might throw a different light on it? That is, could the situation be seen as part of a different issue? Could it be seen as an opportunity in disguise, as a chance to get something different straightened out?

3. **What might you try next?**

What seem to be the central factors in this situation? What are the critical points?

Where are your strengths? How could you use these to respond here?

Can you see one point that might be easier to tackle, control, or find out about than any other? Can you do something about this?

How can you turn your troubles to your advantage?

What are your targets? How much time is required? What are your deadlines and priorities?

What will be the components and who will be the participants of your new situation? Have you specified these?

What are the main functions, operations, or changeable parts?

Where should you expand the most effort and the most time? What area needs the most watching or the most thought?

Which parts should be made to harmonize with each other?

Can you handle all foreseeable emergencies? What are your plans, alternative plans, and priorities?

Must anything else happen to make your plans possible? If so, how will you ensure that they happen?

How do you plan to put your schemes into effect?

Should you do a trial run on this before you finally decide?

How will you check on progress?

Does your plan form a coherent whole? Does it hang together properly?

Can you think of any way to make this more effective? More powerful? More significant?

Can you think of some way to make the plan simpler? Is there a simpler plan than this?

Can you make the plan more flexible?

Can the best part be made better?

Can the worst part be eliminated?

4. Act.
And bear in mind the guidelines in the introduction to this strategy.

5. What do you know now?
Did your action have the required effects? If not, why did it fail? What did you learn from the things that happened?

Have you come by new insights or wisdom as a result of your experiences?

If you succeeded, can your success be improved upon?

Has the action or its effects presented new opportunities? If so, what can be done to exploit these?

Is the action really effective, or are appearances deceiving you?

Did something just happen or change? If so, will it have any effect or not? Where does it fit? What could be done about it?

Should you implement your crisis plan? Do you have a crisis plan? If not, work through Micro-Strategy 6 to devise one.

What new patterns of events might appear?

How might current trends be reinterpreted? What different things might the reinterpretations lead to?

Imagine that the situation, events, or participants are conspiring to surprise you. What might happen? What would be your weakest spot?

What could you do to be ready for this?

What else is going on? Is it significant? Could you connect your situation with this other thing going on, either by discovering subtle links or by making an innovation?

What would happen if the problem situation suddenly deteriorated? Or if it suddenly improved?

If you can foresee something going wrong, how will you handle it, either to prevent it going wrong, or to deal with it afterwards?

Do you have a clearer view of the situation now? What new approaches to your difficulties might this view suggest?

Do any new problems need to be solved? If so, how will you tackle them?

Should you reorganize, rearrange, or reschedule any part of the current effort? Should you change priorities, expand, or contract?

Did you handle this problem in the most effective way? Did you take the best course of action?

Have you learned anything that would enable you to produce better solutions faster in the future?

Did you try to cut out activities that did not contribute directly to overall objectives? Did you concentrate on activities that did?

6. Recommence the cycle.

Now return to 1 of this strategy to define the situation a little more clearly and confidently, and continue this cycle until you can reenter the approach-choosing procedure of Section 6 with a more definite problem description in mind.

Quick-Reference Index of Difficulties and Strategies

DATE DUE			
MY 7 '91			
JA 6 '93			

Sanderson   188508